# The Church Triumphant

## Strategies for War

IRA L. MILLIGAN

Published by:   Servant Ministries, Inc.
                PO Box 1120
                Tioga, LA 71477


ISBN-13: 978-0-9989014-0-4 (paperback)
ISBN-13: 978-0-9989014-1-1 (e-book)

# Acknowledgments

All references to Greek word definitions are from *Strong's Exhaustive Concordance*, Thomas Nelson Publishers, 1990. Unless otherwise noted, all scripture references are taken from the *New King James Version* of the Bible, copyright © 1982 by Thomas Nelson, Inc. Used by permission. All rights reserved.

Scripture quotations marked TPT are taken from *The Psalms: Poetry on Fire*, The Passion Translation, copyright © 2014, 2015,. Used by permission of BroadStreet Publishing Group. LLC, Racine, Wisconsin, USA. All rights reserved.

All Scripture quotations are italicized. When quoting Scripture, the author has sometimes used **bold print** for clarity of expression and for emphasis.

# CONTENTS

# Introduction

Luke records that one day Jesus *"turned to His disciples and said privately, 'Blessed are the eyes which see the things you see; for I tell you that many prophets and kings have desired to see what you see, and have not seen it, and to hear what you hear, and have not heard it'."* (Luke 10:23-24). Once again, we are entering into a time of revelation that God's people have *"desired to see, and have not seen... and to hear... and have not heard"*, but is now being revealed by the Holy Spirit! Paul told the Corinthians *"Eye has not seen, nor ear heard, Nor have entered into the heart of man, The things which God has prepared for those who love Him. But God has revealed them to us through His Spirit"* (1 Corinthians 2:9-10).

Like the disciples of old, we, too, have longed for the day that is just now dawning upon the horizon. But our long wait is coming to an end. That day, with all its power and glory, has arrived. Malachi prophetically summed it up for us in these verses: *"But to you who fear My name The Sun of Righteousness shall arise With healing in His wings; And you shall go out And grow fat like stall-fed calves. You shall trample the wicked, For they shall be ashes under the soles of your feet On the day that I do this, Says the LORD of hosts"* (Malachi 4:2-3). This promise is ours, now — miraculous healings, abundant provision and resounding victory — it is an exciting day to be alive!

Although in times past, most theologians have thought that the Scripture above was referring to the second coming of Christ, upon closer examination of the context, it is obvious that it is actually referring to a specific period of time *before* His return. Malachi continued with, *"Behold, I will send you Elijah the prophet **Before** the coming of the great and dreadful day of the LORD.*

5

# The Church Triumphant

*And he will turn The hearts of the fathers to the children, And the hearts of the children to their fathers, Lest I come and strike the earth with a curse"* (see Malachi 4:5-6).

Malachi's end-time promise, *"You shall trample the wicked, For they shall be ashes under the soles of you feet on the day that I do this"*, corresponds to what Paul promised that God would do *shortly*, *"And the God of peace will crush Satan under your feet shortly. The grace of our Lord Jesus Christ be with you. Amen"* (Romans 16:20). The church has been waiting and longing for Malachi's promise and Paul's "shortly" to come to pass now for many centuries and that wonderful (and awful) day is finally here — wonderful for God's called and chosen — awful for those who reject His call and choose their own way in the face of His offer of boundless grace and tender mercies.

Like the godly disciples who have gone before us in ages pass, we have an indispensable part to play as our Heavenly Father fulfills His eternal, glorious plan to utterly crush and defeat His Son's many enemies. Although this war has been raging for centuries, the final battle has just begun. It's time for God's mighty warriors to rise up and fight alongside their King. So, *"Let God arise, Let His enemies be scattered; Let those also who hate Him flee before Him"* (Psalm 68:1). The following pages outline and unfold numerous strategies and tactics for obtaining a resounding victory in this conflict!

# Chapter One
# The Gospel of the Kingdom

*Wisdom has built her house, She has hewn out her seven pillars... However, the Most High does not dwell in temples made with hands, as the prophet [Isaiah] says: Heaven is My throne, And earth is My footstool. What house will you build for Me? says the LORD, Or what is the place of My rest?* (Proverbs 9:1; Acts 7:48-49)

As Stephen said in the verses above, God doesn't live in church buildings made of brick and stone that we build, rather He dwells in His people. Paul asked the Corinthians *"Do you not know that you are the temple of God and that the Spirit of God dwells in you?"* (1 Corinthians 3:16). God has adopted us into His family, by which we are made citizens of His eternal, everlasting kingdom. He has chosen us and gathered us together for a specific, preordained purpose. He is in the process of building Himself a house—one that will endure forever—a place of everlasting rest and peace! Paul, the apostle to the Gentiles, said, *"Now, therefore, you are no longer strangers and foreigners, but fellow citizens with the saints and members of the household of God, having been built on the foundation of the apostles and prophets, Jesus Christ Himself being the chief corner stone, in whom the whole building, being joined together, grows into a holy temple in the Lord, in whom you also are being built together for a dwelling place of God in the Spirit"* (Ephesians 2:19-22).

Likewise, Peter said that we are all living stones, which, when assembled together constitute both a spiritual house and a holy priesthood for God. He said, *"You also, as living stones, are being built up a spiritual house, a holy priesthood, to offer up spiritual sacrifices acceptable to God through Jesus Christ"* (1 Peter 2:5).

Although the kingdom of God is far greater than the church, encompassing all the earth's inhabitants, God has personally chosen to identify Himself with His church. His ultimate purpose is that both now and in the ages to come He will be glorified in and through His people. They are the permanent, everlasting dwelling that He has chosen to live in. He has predestined that the precious, living stones that He is gathering to build His house with will be glorified with His Son throughout all eternity. Once completed, His house will be exceedingly glorious.

When Moses had the Arc of the Covenant made, which is symbolic of God's first place of residence among His people, he had them overlay it, inside and out, with pure gold. Likewise, when Solomon built the first temple, he overlaid the inside of it with gold. The gold is symbolic of God's magnificent glory (see Haggai 2:6-9).

> *Then Bezalel made the ark of acacia wood... He overlaid it with pure gold inside and outside, and made a molding of gold all around it... So Solomon overlaid the inside of the temple with pure gold. He stretched gold chains across the front of the inner sanctuary, and overlaid it with gold* (Exodus 37:1-2; 1 Kings 6:21)

While many Christians are looking for and expecting the Rapture to occur at any moment, those who understand the signs of the times realize that Christ isn't interested in coming back for the church just yet. Besides being God's house, the church is also the Bride of Christ and He isn't coming back for her before she *"has made herself ready"*, because a husband's bride is his glory! (see Revelations 19:7; 1 Corinthians 11:7). Instead, He is presently in the process of beautifying the church by restoring her to her former purity and beauty.

Although the former, temporal houses that God had men build for Himself were glorious, He has determined that His final, eternal house that *He* is building will be far more beautiful and glorious than those previously made by human hands,

> *For thus saith the LORD of hosts; Yet once, it is a little while, and I will shake the heavens, and the earth, and the sea, and the dry land; And I will shake all nations, and the desire of all nations shall come: and I will fill this house with glory... The silver is mine, and the gold is mine... The glory of this latter house shall be greater than of the former ...and in this place will I give peace, saith the LORD of hosts* (Haggai 2:6-9)

Although in the natural Haggai is referring to the temple of Solomon that was then being rebuilt, his reference to God shaking all nations indicates that this prophecy is really about the end of this age. The first temple was actually symbolic of the church that God is now in the process of rebuilding (much like the first temple was destroyed by the Babylonian king and later rebuilt, the early church was devastated by internal strife and external persecution, and as a result, was brought under the corrupting influence of Roman emperors and ambitious bishops and priests). God is now in the process of recovering all that was lost and stolen and restoring it to even greater power and glory. God has determined that through the church, He will manifest His glory to the ends of the earth. Habakkuk prophesied that

# The Church Triumphant

*"The earth will be filled With the knowledge of the glory of the LORD, As the waters cover the sea"* (Habakkuk 2:14).

Jesus said, *"And this gospel of the kingdom will be preached in all the world as a witness to all the nations, and then the end will come"* (Matthew 24:14). Although much of the world has heard the gospel of salvation, very little of it has heard the gospel of the kingdom or seen it in action! The gospel message preached by Christ and the Apostles was confirmed by miraculous conversions and powerful miracles on a daily basis. We can expect the same results today if we will learn to live by and boldly preach the original message they preached!

Every where that Jesus went He preached the gospel of the kingdom and the results were absolutely phenomenal. Matthew said, *"Jesus went about all the cities and villages, teaching in their synagogues, and preaching the gospel of the kingdom, and healing every sickness and every disease among the people"* (Matthew 9:35).

So what, exactly, is the gospel of the kingdom? What does it offer those who receive it, and what does it require of them? Paul's testimony to the Roman Governor Felix gives us a brief insight into the heart of this message. It also shows that it isn't exactly, *politically correct* or *seeker friendly!*

*And as he reasoned of righteousness, temperance, and judgment to come Felix trembled, and answered, Go thy way for this time; when I have a convenient season, I will call for thee* (Acts 24:25)

The gospel of the kingdom declares that Christ is our Judge, Lawgiver, King *and* Savior, not just our Savior (see Isaiah 33:22). Paul's testimony to Felix and his many epistles to the churches reveal that although righteousness is only obtained by grace through faith in Jesus Christ, that same grace both requires and

10

enables us to walk in true holiness—which is the fruit of walking in temperance and living in moderation—because, as Felix realized and dreaded, all of our deeds will be brought into judgment at Christ's return (see Titus 2:11-12; 2 Corinthians 5:10).

Through Christ's atoning sacrifice God has delivered us from the bondage of the law and the power of sin. Likewise, through His resurrection and the promised outpouring of the Holy Spirit, He has broken the power of tradition and religious legalism. Through this process He has brought us *"into the glorious liberty of the children of God"* (Romans 8:21). But we are not to stop there. We are to go from glory to glory—from one level of glory to the next, in an unending, ever-increasing, upward spiral of glory! Paul said, *"But we all, with unveiled face, beholding as in a mirror the glory of the Lord, are being transformed into the same image from glory to glory, just as by the Spirit of the Lord"* (2 Corinthians 3:18).

We have been liberated from bondage and set free from sin, but there is a difference between *freedom* and *victory*. Moses led the Israelites to freedom—Joshua led them to victory. It is not freedom, but victory that enables us to spoil the strong man and obtain our promised inheritance. Thus, the gospel of salvation gives us freedom from the bondage and defilement of sin but the gospel of the kingdom gives us the authority and power to take back from Satan everything that's been stolen. The Cross of Christ and the promised outpouring of the Holy Spirit has set us free from sin and religious legalism. Now we need to turn our attention toward the next thing on God's agenda —defeating both our enemies and the enemies of our Lord and taking back what belongs to us.

# The Church Triumphant

## The *Full* Gospel

Although many churches call themselves *Full Gospel*, in reality, very few churches minister *the fullness of the blessing of the gospel of Christ*, which would certainly be the case if the full gospel was actually being preached and practiced (see Romans 15:29). We have come up short on ministering the fullness of the blessing because our emphasis has been misplaced. We've preached the gospel of salvation, which is only part of the message, instead of preaching the kingdom of God, which declares the *whole* counsel of God. Luke records that Jesus *"sent them to preach the kingdom of God and to heal the sick"* (Luke 9:2).

The gospel of the kingdom includes the gospel of salvation, but adds a much greater dimension — *resurrection power!* *"For the kingdom of God is not in word but in power"* (1 Corinthians 4:20). God wants us to do more than just talk about His power, He wants us to both live and demonstrate it! Paul reminded the Corinthians that his preaching to them was *"not with persuasive words of human wisdom, but in demonstration of the Spirit and of power, that [their] faith should not be in the wisdom of men but in the power of God"* (1 Corinthians 2:4-5). Our preaching should follow the same pattern if we want the same results!

## Seven Foundational Pillars

Solomon said, *"Wisdom has built her house, She has hewn out her seven pillars"* (Proverbs 9:1). We can see from this verse that God's house should have seven foundational pillars, but the great majority of today's churches, at best, have only four. What are they? (1) Repentance from sin and dead works; (2) Faith in the sacrificial offering of Christ's blood and His resurrection; (3) Water Baptism; (4) and through the Baptism of the Holy Spirit, the Witness of Christ's Resurrection (see 1 Corinthians 15:1-8).

# The Church Triumphant

Together, these four principle doctrines, or "pillars", constitute the gospel of salvation. The full gospel, Biblically known as *"the gospel of the kingdom"*, includes these four but also includes the last three foundational doctrines enumerated in Hebrews: *"Therefore, leaving the discussion of the elementary principles of Christ, let us go on to perfection, not laying again the foundation of repentance from dead works and of faith toward God, of the doctrine of baptisms, of laying on of hands, of resurrection of the dead, and of eternal judgment"* (Hebrews 6:1-2).

In this passage of Scripture the seventh pillar, *perfection (maturity)*, is actually listed first. Perfection is what we are striving for. It is our destiny. As Paul said, we are growing together into a holy temple of the Lord, and our goal is to come into the mature stature of the fullness of Christ: *"Till we all come to the unity of the faith and of the knowledge of the Son of God, to a perfect [mature] man, to the measure of the stature of the fullness of Christ"* (Ephesians 4:13).

So we can interpolate and combine these Scriptures and enumerate the seven foundational pillars of God's house as:

1. Repentance from sin and dead works.
2. Faith toward God and in Christ's atoning works as confirmed by God when He raised Christ from the dead.
3. Water baptism (although, as we will see later, there are actually seven baptisms, of which *water* baptism is only one of the seven).
4. The witness of the resurrection through the baptism of the Holy Spirit and the ministry of the laying on of hands.
5. Resurrection power and authority manifested in and through the church.
6. Eternal judgment administered in the world by the church.

# The Church Triumphant

7. The saints being conformed to the image of the perfect man, the Lord Jesus Christ.

To obey the gospel of salvation, we must die *with* Christ through repentance; be buried *with* Him through water baptism, thus being made dead to the law. Then we must arise *with* Him through faith and walk in newness of life. Lastly, through the baptism of the Holy Spirit, we bear witness of His resurrection as we minister *with* Him through the Laying on of Hands. Notice that in every step we are walking *with* Christ throughout this entire process.

Every complete doctrine has seven precepts, so from the above paragraph it is obvious that three precepts are missing. The gospel of the kingdom includes the above four, but adds the three missing foundational doctrines we saw enumerated in Hebrews Six. The fifth pillar is the *resurrection of the dead* (ascension with its associated power and authority to rule). The sixth is *eternal judgment* (purification—first the church, then the world), and the seventh is *perfection* (mature sons). Just as we followed Christ's example and participated in what He did for us in the first four precepts of the gospel, now it is time to participate with Him in the last three.

Forty days after His resurrection, Jesus ascended to the Father's right hand and will remain there until all His enemies are made His footstool. David exclaimed, *"The LORD said to my Lord, "Sit at My right hand, Till I make Your enemies Your footstool." The LORD shall send the rod of Your strength out of Zion. Rule in the midst of Your enemies!"* (Psalm 110:1-2). And by whom are His enemies to be defeated and made His footstool? By no one else but you and me, the children of God! And how is this going to be accomplished? Exactly the way God said it would. Through the blood of the Lamb, the word of our testimony, and by our total, radical devotion and commitment to God,

> *And war broke out in [the second] heaven... and Satan, who deceives the whole world; he was cast to the earth, and his angels were cast out with him. Then I heard a loud voice saying in heaven, 'Now salvation, and strength,* **and the kingdom of our God, and the power of His Christ have come**, *for the accuser of our brethren, who accused them before our God day and night, has been cast down. And they overcame him by the blood of the Lamb and by the word of their testimony, and they did not love their lives to the death'* (see Revelation 12:7-11)

This war has raged for centuries, but the victory is near. God is presently equipping us with the knowledge and power to enable us to win this war. He is in the process of answering Paul's prayer for the Ephesians (representative of the whole church). He prayed for them (and us) to have the revelation of what God originally purposed to manifest in and though them—the fullness of His resurrection power and glory. Paul prayed for the Ephesians to receive, *"the spirit of wisdom and revelation in the knowledge of Him... that you may know... what is the exceeding greatness of His power toward us who believe, according to the working of His mighty power which He worked in Christ when He raised Him from the dead and seated Him at His right hand in the heavenly places"* (see Ephesians 1:16-23).

Previously, we've discussed how we follow Christ in fulfilling the first four precepts of the gospel. Our next assignment is to ascend *with* Christ by faith into the heavenly places and rule *with* Him over the darkness of this present, evil age. Paul said that God has *"raised us up together, and made us sit together in the heavenly places in Christ Jesus"* (Ephesians 2:6).

To obey the *full* gospel, we must ascend into the heavenly places with Christ to rule over the darkness of this world. In the beginning God made two great lights, the greater light to rule the day, the lesser light to rule the night (see Genesis 1:14-19). Jesus is the light of the world, ruling over the day. In Him there is no darkness at all. He is as the sun shining in its strength. Likewise, God created the church to rule over the night. Although the gospel of salvation liberates the church *from* darkness, it doesn't automatically make her victorious *over* darkness. It takes resurrection power imparted through the *Baptism of Fire* to accomplish that, and that is exactly what God is preparing the church to receive!

Paul prophesied that the day was coming when God was going to crush Satan under our feet. He promised, *"And the God of peace will crush Satan under your feet shortly"* (Romans 16:20). The Greek word *syntribo,* which is translated *crush* in this Scripture, means *"to render an utter, crushing defeat"* (Strong's 4937). The church has been waiting and longing for God to fulfill that prophetic promise for centuries, and that day has finally arrived. The time is now!

John the Baptist said that Jesus was going to baptize His disciples with the Holy Spirit *and* Fire. The baptism of Fire, which consists of *resurrection power and purification,* is a necessary impartation and anointing for us to be able to fulfill Paul's prophetic promise and to complete the Great Commission that Jesus gave us. This promised baptism is presently on God's agenda,

# The Church Triumphant

*John answered, saying to all, 'I indeed baptize you with water; but One mightier than I is coming, whose sandal strap I am not worthy to loose. He will baptize you with the Holy Spirit and fire. His winnowing fan is in His hand, and He will thoroughly clean out His threshing floor, and gather the wheat into His barn; but the chaff He will burn with unquenchable fire.'* (Luke 3:16-17)

The baptism of the Holy Spirit is a present reality, of which millions of God's people are partakers. A fresh outpouring of the baptism of Fire is next. Without it, we cannot accomplish what God has purposed to do from the beginning, which is to bring the whole world into accountability before He sends His Son back to punish the wicked and be glorified in His people. Paul encouraged the Thessalonians, who were being persecuted for their faith, with this assurance,

*And to give you who are troubled rest with us when the Lord Jesus is revealed from heaven with His mighty angels, in flaming fire taking vengeance on those who do not know God, and on those who do not obey the gospel of our Lord Jesus Christ. These shall be punished with everlasting destruction from the presence of the Lord and from the glory of His power, when He comes... to be glorified in His saints and to be admired among all those who believe, because our testimony among you was believed* (2 Thessalonians 1:7-10)

It's time to come up higher. It's time to ascend into the heavens with Christ and assume our kingly role. It's time to rule with the King!

# The Church Triumphant

# Chapter Two
# Kingdom Fundamentals

When Jesus taught the multitudes about the kingdom of God, He always spoke in parables. In one of His many illustrious parables, He said, *"The kingdom of God is as if a man should scatter seed on the ground, and should sleep by night and rise by day, and the seed should sprout and grow, he himself does not know how. For the earth yields crops by itself: first the blade, then the head, after that the full grain in the head. But when the grain ripens, immediately he puts in the sickle, because the harvest has come"* (Mark 4:26-29).

This parable reveals several important truths about the kingdom of God, three in particular. First, notice the *process*. The kingdom must be planted and allowed to grow before its fruits can be enjoyed. The Bible admonishes us to *"be not slothful, but followers of those who through faith and patience inherit the promises"* (Hebrews 6:12). You can't "hurry" nature, nor can you speed up the kingdom! You have to patiently yield to the process.

The second fundamental truth is this, we should *rest in the promises* (not toss and turn all night), because God isn't going to do anything the way we expect Him to, nor is He operating on our time-table. He strictly operates on His own! The seed (God's Word) will *"sprout and grow"* when the conditions are right, and if we give it the necessary nutrients (make the necessary sacrifices of time and substance), it will bear fruit in the due process of time.

The third fundamental principle is this, *"when the grain ripens, immediately he puts in the sickle"*. After what seems like a long wait things suddenly come to a head, and if we aren't watching expectantly, we will miss the hour of our visitation. Ripened fruit perishes quickly. We have to be careful not to be distracted or become complacent and lose our blessings. Jesus warned the church to always be alert and watching for His return. Things can come to fruition and change rather suddenly!

Although the kingdom of God is greater than the church, Christ's true church is the only visible, tangible, recognizable expression of the kingdom in the earth. God owns this world and although Satan obtained control of it through Adam's blunder, God sent His Son to raise up and lead a revolutionary army to reconquer it. God's army is His church. Jesus' introduction of the church in the *Gospel of Matthew* both implies war and declares victory! When He first met Peter, He told him, *"And I also say to you that you are Peter, and on this rock I will build My church, and the gates of Hades shall not prevail against it"* (Matthew 16:18).

Jesus openly declared war on the kingdom of darkness from the onset, assuring us of victory even before leading us into battle! He illustrated this in the beginning of His ministry. When Satan foolishly challenged Him to a duel in the wilderness, Jesus utterly defeated him, taking back the crown he had stolen from Adam in the process.

How could Jesus be so sure of victory, both then and now? Because both He and His people have this promise: *"The LORD will cause your enemies who rise against you to be defeated before your face; they shall come out against you one way and flee before you seven ways"* (Deuteronomy 28:7). This promise of resounding victory, along with every other positive promise in the Old Covenant, is included in the New Covenant that we operate under.

Paul said, *"For you were once darkness, but now you are light in the Lord"* (Ephesians 5:8). Light totally dominates and utterly obliterates darkness—no exception! On the forth day of creation *"God made two great lights: the greater light [Jesus] to rule the day, and the lesser light [the church] to rule the night. God set them in the heavens to rule over the day and over the night, and to divide the light from the darkness"* (Genesis 1:16-18). We were created to rule!

Jesus introduced the kingdom of God with this command, *"The time is fulfilled, and the kingdom of God is at hand. Repent, and believe in the gospel"* (Mark 1:15). Many look forward to Christ's return in anticipation of experiencing His kingdom during the Millennium reign. But Jesus said the kingdom was already here, at hand, to be received and occupied along with many (but not all) of its accompanying benefits. During the Millennium reign God will supernaturally impose many important changes to this present world order (the discussion of these changes are beyond the scope of this book). Nevertheless, if we consider the many promises and benefits of the kingdom of God as strictly being for the regeneration to come, we are making a serious blunder and depriving ourselves of His promised blessings.

Before Paul went to Rome he assured the Romans, *"I know that when I come to you, I shall come in the fullness of the blessing of the gospel of Christ"* (Romans 15:29). So, how do we enter into His kingdom and obtain the *"fullness of the blessing of the gospel"*? Simply by doing what Jesus said, repent, believe and obey the gospel. Why add *obey* to this command? Because those who truly believe, obey. It isn't just faith but rather the expression of our faith through obedience that qualifies us to partake of the many, precious benefits. As Isaiah said, *"If you are willing and obedient, You shall eat the good of the land"* (Isaiah 1:19).

Today, many reject this simple admonition, stating that everything is by faith, alone, but James said *"Faith without works is dead"* and Paul said, *"the gospel was made known to all nations for the obedience of faith*" (see James 2:20; Romans 16:26). God's grace gives us the faith not only to believe Him but also to obey Him and our obedience releases His blessings. Jesus was and is a man of perfect faith. He is both our pattern to emulate and our example to follow. He said, *"And He who sent Me is with Me. The Father has not left Me alone, for I always do those things that please Him"* (John 8:29).

God's ways never change. When God revealed His ways and purpose to the Israelites, those who believed Him fought and conquered their enemies, thus they received and enjoyed their promised inheritance. Those who refused to believe and fight wandered aimlessly in the wilderness without ever enjoying what God promised to give them. As Jesus said, *"The kingdom of heaven suffers violence, and the violent [believe, obey and] take it by force"* (Matthew 11:12).

As stated above, Paul said, *"I know that when I come to you, I shall come in the fullness of the blessing of the gospel of Christ"* (Romans 15:29). What is the fullness of the blessing of the gospel? Peter summed up all the benefits and blessings in one long sentence, *"Grace and peace be multiplied to you in the knowledge of God and of Jesus our Lord, as His divine power has given to us all things that pertain to life and godliness, through the **knowledge** of Him who called us by glory and virtue"* (2 Peter 1:2-3).

But there's a problem. The Greek word *epignosis,* translated *knowledge* in this passage of Scripture means *experiential* knowledge, not just intellectual knowledge. To receive the fullness of the blessings of the gospel, one must truly know Christ, not just know about Him.

Unlike the popular, "seeker-sensitive, hyper-grace" gospel that many ministers are embracing today, those who truly follow Christ and walk with God know that serving Christ isn't always a "walk in the park". They also know Him as one who is *"despised and rejected by men, a Man of sorrows and acquainted with grief"* (Isaiah 53:3). In fact, Paul said, *"If in this life only we have hope in Christ, we are of all men the most pitiable"* (1 Corinthians 15:19). God will reward the faithful for their service, suffering and sacrifice, not just for attending church. God is searching for those who will forsake this world's comforts and pleasures and walk with Him, regardless of the cost.

When Peter asked Jesus what the future held for himself and his fellow disciples, Jesus responded with, *"Assuredly, I say to you, there is no one who has left house or brothers or sisters or father or mother or wife or children or lands, for My sake and the gospel's, who shall not receive a hundredfold now in this time—houses and brothers and sisters and mothers and children and lands, with persecutions—and in the age to come, eternal life"* (see Mark 10:28-30).

Jesus told His disciples to *"seek the kingdom of God, and all these [natural] things shall be added to you. Do not fear, little flock, for it is your Father's good pleasure to give you the kingdom"* (Luke 12:31-32). So, who is the kingdom given to and how is it received? It is bestowed upon everyone who obeys and serves God, and it is received with simple, childlike faith. Jesus said, *"Assuredly... whoever does not receive the kingdom of God as a little child will by no means enter it"* (Mark 10:15).

## Two Parallel Universes

It is interesting to note that modern scientists speculate about the possibility of parallel universes, whether they exist or not. They do exist, but probably not as they think. In a very real sense there are two, distinct, parallel universes that occupy the same space and time. These two interact with each other in specific, predictable ways. One consists of the kingdoms of this world; the other is the kingdom of Heaven. One natural, the other spiritual. One corruptible, the other incorruptible. One temporary, the other eternal. One is visible, the other invisible. The invisible one existed before the visible, and the Creator of both is the King who exercises dominion over all things.

God rules over both universes and holds everyone accountable for his or her deeds in the visible universe and every spirit accountable in the invisible (both angels and demons). He will bring all things into eternal judgment after He combines the two universes into one, united, visible reality, executing equitable judgment and justice for everyone, including the angels and demons.

God's servants are chosen out of this world to represent Him as His ambassadors and judges. Before we can exercise our God given authority we must first renounce our former citizenship with this world and acknowledge our heavenly citizenship that we obtained when we were born-again (see John 17:15-18; Philippians 3:20).

Because we were born in this world, we are citizens of the world. But when we died with Christ in repentance and were born-again through faith in His resurrection, we forsook this world's citizenship and became citizens of God's eternal kingdom. As long as we live as citizens of this world we are subject to its laws and restrictions. To what extent we hold onto its temporal advantages, to that extent we are denied access to the fullness of God's eternal, spiritual blessings. Paul said that we must, *"Come out from among them And be separate, says the Lord. Do not touch what is unclean, And I will receive you. I will be a Father to you, And you shall be My sons and daughters, Says the LORD Almighty"* (2 Corinthians 6:17-18).

# The Church Triumphant

A recent news broadcast (2016) showed pictures of armed Muslim extremist persecuting and executing Christians, including children, which motivated several Christian viewers to comment fearfully that the world was going to get much worse before it gets better. The problem with this view is their faith is in what they are seeing and hearing instead of being in agreement with what the Word of God clearly promises!

There is no scripture anywhere in the Bible that shows a Muslim takeover of the world in the last days. Christ is set to take over through the church, not Satan through Islam! *"God, who gives life to the dead and calls those things which do not exist as though they did"*, has declared the end from the beginning, and in the beginning He said the woman's Seed would crush Satan's head! (see Romans 4:17; Genesis 3:15). As we saw previously, Paul echoed these words with, *"And the God of peace shall crush Satan under your feet shortly"* (Romans 16:20). We should be expecting a church takeover, not an Islamic takeover (though not by force and coercion, as they do). Regardless of what all the news anchors are reporting and the doomsday prophets are declaring, we have the more sure word of prophecy that promises us that through Christ, we will prevail!

So, the King, the kingdom and the church—how do they relate, and what about timing? Obviously, the church is for today, but what about the King and the kingdom? Are they here now, or yet to come? Jesus told Peter that he was going to be instrumental in building His church, and in the very next verse He spoke of giving him the keys to the kingdom, implying that the church and the kingdom were closely related and would coexist. Also, when Pilate asked Christ if He was King of the Jews, He answered in the affirmative, showing that even as the kingdom presently exists, He both was and is its King (see Matthew 16:18-19; 2:2; 27:11).

And the church? How does it relate? The church is Christ's agent to proclaim, establish and manifest His kingdom here on the earth. Therefore the church has the responsibility to manifest Christ as both the sacrificial Lamb of God and as the reigning Lion of the Tribe of Judah. The church is responsible to present Christ as both suffering servant and reigning King—not just as the sacrificial Lamb of God. He is far more than that!

This involves a paradigm shift in the way the church has believed and operated in the past. As the Lamb, Christ mercifully saves and delivers. But as the Lion, which is the "king of beasts", He rules, judges and conquers, crushing His enemies and making them His footstool. His divine nature never changes (see Psalm 110:1-3: Revelation 19:11).

The compassionate, merciful aspect of His nature in no way overrides or annuls the fiery manifestation of His wrath. God is Love, but He is also a Consuming Fire. Jesus is coming back, indeed, just as everyone is expecting, but this time He's coming back with flaming, burning, consuming Fire! (see 2 Thessalonians 1:7-9; Hebrews 12:29)

As we stated above, God's kingdom is greater than the church. We've discussed how the kingdom of God relates to the church, now we need to turn our attention to how it relates to the citizens of the kingdom. First, if you are a born-again child of God, Jesus is both your Lord and your King, but the same may not be true concerning your neighbor. Though he may not acknowledge Jesus as his Lord, Jesus is still his King, regardless of how he feels about the matter. The reason is Jesus Christ is the King of kings and Lord of lords. He is sovereign, having all power in heaven and earth. Scripture tells us that *"The earth is the LORD'S, and all its fullness, The world and those who dwell therein"* (Psalm 24:1).

Although a nation's citizens may appoint a king over themselves, nevertheless, God assures us, *"The king's heart is in the hand of the LORD, Like the rivers of water; He turns it wherever He wishes"* (Proverbs 21:1). Kings, dictators and presidents only *think* they are in charge! Paul said, *"there is no authority except from God, and the authorities that exist are appointed by God"* (Romans 13:1). Since they are given their authority by God, they are accountable for how they use it to God. He's their boss!

The church's job isn't to bring the kingdom to the earth—it is already here—our job is to make the world's inhabitants aware that Jesus is its King and that one day He will administer judgment and justice to all. David said, *"But the Lord shall endure forever; He has prepared His throne for judgment. He shall judge the world in righteousness, And He shall administer judgment for the peoples in uprightness"* (Psalm 9:7-8), And Solomon summed up the book of Ecclesiastes with, *"For God shall bring every work into judgment, with every secret thing, whether it be good, or whether it be evil"* (Ecclesiastes 12:14).

Jesus sits upon the Throne of David, and *"David reigned over all Israel, and administered judgment and justice to all his people"* (1 Chronicles 18:14). Does this mean that everyone under David's rule in Israel received prompt, fair justice when they were wronged, even to the furthest reaches of the kingdom? Obviously not—only those cases that were brought to the king's attention. Likewise, although King Jesus has been given the throne of David, and on judgment day all things will be judged by Him, until then, only those cases that are specifically brought to His attention are judged (see Luke 1:31-33; John 5:22).

# The Church Triumphant

Many of the citizens of the kingdom of God are living under oppressive and grievous circumstances because they don't understand this principal. They are unaware that the King is more than willing to judge their cases if they were brought before Him in prayer. God instructs us to *"Put Me in remembrance; Let us contend together; State your case, that you may be acquitted"* (Isaiah 43:26).

For those who think that since this is in the Old Testament it isn't necessary today, notice that Jesus gave us a parable teaching us the exact same thing in the New Testament,

> *Then He spoke a parable to them, that men always ought to pray and not lose heart saying: There was in a certain city a judge... Now there was a widow in that city; and she came to him, saying, 'Get justice for me from my adversary.' ...shall God not avenge His own elect who cry out day and night to Him, though He bears long with them? I tell you that He will avenge them speedily. Nevertheless, when the Son of Man comes, will He really find faith on the earth?* (Luke 18:1-3,7-8)

Jesus is Lord, yet He does not operate on His own agenda. He only does His Father's will. He allowed John the Baptist to be beheaded without interfering in any way (see Luke 3:19-20, 7:19,22-23). Likewise, He allowed James to be beheaded by Herod and would have allowed Peter to suffer the same fate if the church had not woke up and started praying for his protection (see Acts 12:1-12). We should be under no allusion that Christ will make an exception in our case. Jesus is the majestic King of kings and Lord of lords. He simply will not bow to our expectations or give in to our demands, but He does respond to our humble prayers and supplications.

# Chapter Three
# Christ the King

*Now I saw heaven opened, and behold, a white horse. And He who sat on him was called Faithful and True, and in righteousness He judges and makes war... And He has on His robe and on His thigh a name written: KING OF KINGS AND LORD OF LORDS* (Revelation 19:11,16)

What are kings for? What are they supposed to do? The answer to those two questions will reveal God's final thrust in the world through the church.

When Israel cried out for God to give them a king, Samuel warned them that they really didn't know what they were asking for, but in spite of his warning, *"Nevertheless the people refused to obey the voice of Samuel; and they said, Nay; but we will have a king [to rule] over us; That we also may be like all the nations; and that our king may judge us, and go out before us, and fight our battles"* (1 Samuel 8:19-20).

They said they wanted a king to rule over them, judge them and fight their battles for them. We can see from this that kings *rule, judge* and *wage war*. These three things describe the kingdom of God in action! We will expand and expound upon these three roles as we continue but first we need to define *kingdom* because it has more than one possible meaning. George Eldon Ladd, in his excellent book titled, *The Gospel of the Kingdom*, defined the word kingdom in this way: "The *primary* meaning of both the Hebrew word *malkuth* in the Old Testament and of the Greek word *basileia* in the New Testament is the rank, authority and sovereignty exercised by a king [so, he concluded that] first of all, a kingdom is the authority to rule, the sovereignty of the king" (page 19).

Since a king's rule would be meaningless if he didn't have someone to rule over, the word can also include the king's subjects and the realm over which he rules, but as Ladd observed, the *primary* meaning is to rule—and this is obviously what Christ had in mind when He responded to the Pharisees' question about the kingdom,

> *Now when He was asked by the Pharisees when the kingdom of God would come, He answered them and said, "The kingdom of God does not come with observation; nor will they say, 'See here!' or 'See there!' For indeed, the kingdom of God is within you"* (Luke 17:20-21)

God rules His subjects from within, not from without. Under the Old Covenant (the Ten Commandments), God's law was written on tablets of stone. Under the New Covenant, He writes His law in our hearts. Paul exhorted the Philippians to *"work out your own salvation with fear and trembling; for it is God who works in you both to will and to do His good pleasure"* (Philippians 2:12-13).

Although we should certainly fear God, His kingdom rule does not consists of an overbearing, authoritarian dictatorship. Instead, God rules with the benevolent rule of a loving Father! But, if God is love, as we have been taught (and He is), why did Paul say that we should walk before Him with *"fear and trembling"*? The answer is simple. We should fear Him because He chastens those whom He loves, *"For whom the LORD loves He chastens, And scourges every son whom He receives"* (Hebrews 12:6).

# The Church Triumphant

To avoid being chastened, we must be obedient, and as Paul told the Philippians, the Holy Spirit guides us from within, not from without. We do not please God by adhering to a strict set of religious laws and holiness standards. If religious laws and rules worked, God would not have released us from the requirement to observe Moses' law. God has written His law in our hearts, not on stone as He did under the law's dispensation. Moses gave Israel over six hundred laws. When Jesus came He reduced them down to only two. When a lawyer asked Him which commandment of the law was the greatest, He answered with, *"You shall love the LORD your God with all your heart, with all your soul, and with all your mind" This is the first and great commandment. And the second is like it: "You shall love your neighbor as yourself." On these two commandments hang all the Law and the Prophets"* (Matthew 22:36-40). Likewise, Paul tells us, *"For all the law is fulfilled in one word, even in this: 'You shall love your neighbor as yourself'."* (Galatians 5:14). That one word is *love*. Jesus said that when we put love into action by treating others the same way we want to be treated, we are fulfilling the requirements of both the law and the prophets (see Matthew 7:12).

## Ruling with Christ

It is very important that we understand and grasp this concept of walking in love because God wants us to rule with Him, and to do so it is imperative that we have the Father's heart. To be able to walk in harmony with Him we have to know what manner of Spirit He operates by. John and James discovered this when Jesus was rejected by the Samaritans,

*And as they went, they entered a village of the Samaritans, to prepare for Him. But they did not receive Him, because His face*

*was set for the journey to Jerusalem. And when His disciples James and John saw this, they said, 'Lord, do You want us to command fire to come down from heaven and consume them, just as Elijah did?' But He turned and rebuked them, and said, 'You do not know what manner of spirit you are of. For the Son of Man did not come to destroy men's lives but to save them.' And they went to another village* (Luke 9:52-56)

Christ sits upon the throne of David and although David certainly wasn't perfect in all his ways, he had one great, redeeming trait—he was known as *"a man after God's own heart"* (see 1 Samuel 13:14). We don't have to be immaculate to rule with Christ, but we do have to learn the meaning of mercy! Jesus said, *"go and learn what this means, 'I desire mercy and not sacrifice'."* (Matthew 9:13).

Those who abuse their authority and rule with heavy–handed tactics and exercise lordship over their brethren are not representing Christ. He does not work that way. They are operating in witchcraft and sorcery! God doesn't condone the abuse of His children. Jesus said that in His kingdom the ones who were esteemed the greatest among them would be those who served the others,

*Now there was also a dispute among them, as to which of them should be considered the greatest. And He said to them, 'The kings of the Gentiles exercise lordship over them, and those who exercise authority over them are called 'benefactors.' But not so among you; on the contrary, he who is greatest among you, let him be as the younger, and he who governs as he who serves'* (Luke 22:24-26)

# The Church Triumphant

Peter addressed this concept in his first epistle when he addressed the elders of the church. (He also mentioned the glorious reward that awaits Christ's shepherds if they are faithful to serve the people in the manner that God has instructed them to do),

*The elders who are among you I exhort... Shepherd the flock of God which is among you, serving as overseers, not by compulsion but willingly, not for dishonest gain but eagerly; nor as being lords over those entrusted to you, but being examples to the flock; and when the Chief Shepherd appears, you will receive the crown of glory that does not fade away* (1 Peter 5:1-4)

In the Olivetti discourse, shortly before He was crucified, Jesus gave His disciples a promise of great reward if they were faithful in carrying out their duties as He had taught them to. He gave them instructions on how to properly perform their duties as *"ruler over his household"*. He also warned them not to abuse the authority He was entrusting them with,

*Who then is a faithful and wise servant, whom his master made* **ruler over his household***, to give them food in due season? Blessed is that servant whom his master, when he comes, will find so doing. Assuredly, I say to you that he will make him ruler over all his goods. But if that evil servant says in his heart, 'My master is delaying his coming,' and begins to beat his fellow servants, and to eat and drink with the drunkards, the master of that servant will come on a day when he is not looking for him and at an hour that he is not aware of, and will cut him in two and appoint him his portion with the hypocrites. There shall be weeping and gnashing of teeth* (Matthew 24:45-51)

# The Church Triumphant

Peter said that we, *"as living stones, are being built up a spiritual house, a holy priesthood, to offer up spiritual sacrifices acceptable to God through Jesus Christ"* (1 Peter 2:5). Likewise John said that Christ has *"redeemed us to God by Your blood... And have made us kings and priests to our God; And we shall reign on the earth"* (Revelation 5:9-10). The church has faithfully offered up spiritual sacrifices of intercession, praise and thanksgiving, thereby ministering as holy *"priests to our God"* but has utterly failed to *"reign on the earth"* as spiritual kings with Him.

Although in the past we have seen reigning with Christ as a future promise to be fulfilled only in the Millennium, we need to take a closer look at what John actually said. Quite obviously, the priesthood ministry that both Peter and John spoke of are for this present age, not the Millennium. Likewise, even as our ministry as priests is actually Christ's Priesthood manifested in and through us, so in like manner His Kingly rule is conducted through us! The Bible says that we ,*"have tasted the good word of God and the powers of the age to come [and] Where the word of a king is, there is power"* (Hebrews 6:5; Ecclesiastes 8:4). God desires to release *"the word of a King"* and demonstrate His mighty power through us! Without our participation there is practically no recognizable, visible manifestation of His rule to be seen!

Jesus told the apostles, *"And I bestow upon you a kingdom, just as My Father bestowed one upon Me"* (Luke 22:29). And in what manner has the Father bestowed the kingdom upon His Son? By giving Him unlimited *spiritual* authority over His entire creation, and has appointed a day in which He will rule with unlimited *natural* authority over all the kingdoms of this world. We must learn to distinguish between spiritual authority and natural authority. There is a difference. Although our natural authority is limited to the natural things that we are responsible for, Jesus has given us tremendous spiritual authority that covers many kingdom issues and areas that we have either neglected out of ignorance or have been reluctant to operate in.

For example, Jesus chose seventy of His followers and *"sent them two by two before His face into every city and place where He Himself was about to go"* (Luke 10:1-2). After they completed their mission and returned to give their report, they expressed surprise and were excited about the fact that they had far more power and authority than they had previously realized,

> *Then the seventy returned with joy, saying, 'Lord, even the demons are subject to us in Your name.' And He said to them, 'I saw Satan fall like lightning from heaven. Behold, I give you the authority to trample on serpents and scorpions, and over all the power of the enemy, and nothing shall by any means hurt you'* (Luke 10:17-19)

Christ is King over the spiritual kingdom now (the kingdom of God), and will rule as King over all the natural kingdoms of this world during the Millennium. Likewise, we are rulers with Him over the spiritual kingdom now and we will be rulers over the natural, earthly kingdoms with Him during the Millennium (see Revelation 20:6).

When Jesus told the apostles, *"I bestow upon you a kingdom, just as My Father bestowed one upon Me"* (Luke 22:29), He was bequeathing the spiritual authority that His Father had given Him unto them, much as King David, shortly before his death, passed the natural crown to govern Israel to Solomon (see 1 Kings 1:32-35). Through this process, both King David and Jesus endeavored to assure the kingdoms that they had fought so valiantly to establish would continue, unbroken and unabated.

# The Church Triumphant

The confusion in differentiating between the spiritual and natural kingdoms' manifestations has given rise to the phrase, "kingdom now—kingdom not yet". In reality, God's kingdom has always existed in the now, but not to the necked eye. Actually, the phrase should be, *spiritual, invisible kingdom* now—*natural, visible kingdom,* not yet—but in its proper time it will be both natural and visible. As in so many other aspects of God's creative works, there is an every increasing revelation of His eternal purpose as He unfolds His plans. But Isaiah prophesied that once God revealed the mystery of His kingdom, His government would never cease to increase,

*Of the increase of His government and peace There will be no end, Upon the throne of David and over His kingdom, To order it and establish it with judgment and justice From that time forward, even forever. The zeal of the LORD of hosts will perform this* (Isaiah 9:7)

Jesus both declared the kingdom (His rule), and demonstrated it. He said, *"...if I cast out demons by the Spirit of God, surely the kingdom of God has come upon you"* (Matthew 12:28). The promised increase of Christ's reign that Isaiah prophesied of began with Jesus' ministry and, to one degree or another, has continued to manifest in and through the church ever since. When Jesus walked the earth, at best a few thousand souls were added to the kingdom. Since then, millions have been added and millions more will be as this age draws to a close.

During His earthly ministry the Jews failed to recognize the kingdom because they were looking for its natural manifestation instead of its spiritual manifestation. When Jesus faced Pilate, He said, *"My kingdom is not of this world. If My kingdom were of this* *world, My servants would fight, so that I should not be delivered to the Jews; but **now** My kingdom is not from here"* (John 18:36).

*Now*, His kingdom is not from this world. It is *in* the world, but it is not *of* it. *Now* it is a spiritual kingdom, but *then*, a natural one. The spiritual kingdom is, *at hand*, now. Now, at this time, it is a present-tense reality. Mark said that after John the Baptist was put in prison, *"Jesus came to Galilee, preaching the gospel of the kingdom of God, and saying, 'The time is fulfilled, and the kingdom of God is at hand. Repent, and believe in the gospel"* (Mark 1:14-15).

*"The time is fulfilled and the kingdom of God is at hand"*! Now, Jesus is a *"life-giving Spirit"*, giving eternal life to all that confess Him as their Lord and Savior and willingly submit to Him as their King (see 1 Corinthians 15:45). Now, all submission is voluntary. But, during the Millennium, He will *"rule with a rod of iron"*, and all who will not willingly submit to Him will be slain before His face (see Revelation 19:15; Luke 19:27). But now His rule takes on a different form. Although it has many natural manifestations, at present it is spiritual in both its power and its application.

David prophesied that *"The LORD shall send the rod of Your strength out of Zion. Rule in the midst of Your enemies! Your people shall be volunteers In the day of Your power"* (Psalm 110:2-3). At this time the rod of Christ's strength isn't being sent out of natural Zion but it *is* being sent out of spiritual Zion. There is a natural Mount Zion, in Israel, and there is a spiritual Mount Zion that is far greater in glory, which is the church (see Hebrews 12:22-23).

This Psalm applies to this present age, not to the future. How can this be determined? First, David spoke of ruling in the midst of Christ's enemies. During the Millennium there are no enemies present! Satan is bound and cast into Hell during that dispensation (he isn't released until near the end). Second, during the Millennium, Christ's rule is with a rod of iron. He won't be asking for volunteers—He will be issuing commands! Thus Isaiah is saying that we are supposed to wield *the rod of His strength* and demonstrate it now, in this present evil age. This scripture is not referring to some time in the distant future. The time is fulfilled. The kingdom is now at hand.

So, what does Christians ruling with kingly, spiritual authority look like? Jesus delegated the highest level of spiritual authority in His kingdom to the apostles (see Matthew 10:1,8). So, what does apostolic authority actually consist of? We will examine that more throughly when we get into the actual strategies of waging effective, spiritual warfare, but first it is necessary to examine the upcoming, third reformation and how it relates to the new apostles and their ministry.

# Chapter Four
# The Third Reformation

When home groups, or cell groups, as they are commonly called, were first reintroduced into America's church culture in the latter part of the twentieth century, the question was raised, "Are cell groups the next move of God?" Of course, the answer is no; cell groups are but one of God's many instruments to facilitate the next move but they are not the move itself. Cell groups are a form of ministry designed to facilitate a much needed function but it is important to note that *regardless of how effective and important the form is, the form is never equal to the function.* To equate the two invariably leads to error.

God's next move contains far more than just another way of doing church. In fact, it is rather complex, because it both embodies all that has gone before it, plus it adds a new, and heretofore missing dimension to "doing church," as we presently know and experience in our services.

God's next move has four separate, but fully interrelated characteristics: First, this new move requires *a change in church government*. Although attempting to change the way the church is governed will invariably result in a reformation, it is absolutely necessary because the complete restoration of apostolic government and ministry simply cannot be implemented using the existing system that we have inherited from our forefathers. Second, this move incorporates *a new emphasis on evangelism* that is, for the most part, completely missing at present. Third, it replaces the casual acquaintances that are developed between the brethren using the present structure with *koinonia* (intimate fellowship and real relationships among the brethren), and last, but certainly not least, before it can succeed *all of God's people must get involved in the work.*

Jesus gave us a command to *"Go... into all the world, and preach the gospel to every creature"* (Mark 16:15), and that mandate simply cannot be fulfilled without everyone working together to accomplish it. Of course, this is where cell groups come into the picture. We will never evangelize all the world without the whole church getting involved—and even that's not enough. The task is simply too large for the present untrained, unmotivated work force to complete.

It's not hard to see that it would be difficult to accomplish any one of these tasks using the form that is presently in use, and to fulfill all four would simply be impossible. And of the four, although it isn't at first apparent, the change in government is the key to this new move's ultimate success. As we mentioned earlier, changing the church's government will require another reformation. Nevertheless, if the church doesn't function according to the proper biblical pattern, it cannot accomplish all that God expects it to.

The twenty-first century started out with much uncertainty (remember the "Y-2-K" doomsayers?) and major change—introduced, in part, by the terrorist attack on 9/11/2001. But the church was already being shaken before either of those two events transpired. The latter part of the twentieth century saw many churches experiencing stagnation and negative growth as dissatisfied and disgruntled Christians left their ranks to gather in private homes for worship and fellowship.

After King Solomon died, his arrogant son tried to impose a strict, intolerant rule upon the Israelites. Their response was illustrative to what the church has encountered during the last two or three decades, *"Now when all Israel saw that the king did not listen to them, the people answered the king, saying: 'What share have we in David?...To your tents, O Israel! Now, see to your own house, O David!' So Israel departed to their tents"* (1 Kings 12:16).

Church history reveals that this pattern of dissatisfaction with stagnant, restrictive and sometimes even abusive church government—which results in the people separating themselves from the established churches and regrouping into small home groups while they wait for change in the leadership structure—has been repeated for generations. It was going on even before Martin Luther kicked off the reformation in 1517 and their use was one reason John Wesley's ministry was so effective in the 1700s (cell groups were called *classes*).

Every time God wants to bring His people into a new level of spirituality He has to call them out of the old so that He can bring them into the new (the Greek word *ekklesia*, translated *church* in Scripture, literally means "called out"). This explains the broad popularity of the current "house church" or "cell church" movement.

Usually, after a season this pattern of migration is followed by the people reforming into new patterns of public worship and spiritual service. This gradual shift from small, informal gatherings toward more structured worship is happening at this present time.

When David went to get the Ark of the Covenant (which represents God's manifest presence) and restore it to its rightful place, he placed it upon a new ox-cart—as the Philistines had done years before—and happily headed for Jerusalem. When the oxen stumbled God killed one of the drivers. David quickly realized that he was in error and took the Ark aside into the house of a Levite named Obed-Edom. Obed means *worker* and Edom means *red*, which further translates to *passion*. Thus, the manifest presence of God was awarded to a family who *had a passion to work for God*. The Ark with its associated spiritual blessings of abundant provision remained there for three months. Three means *conformed*.

Once David recognized his error and understood and conformed to God's proper order he returned for the Ark and this time, God gave him good success. Once the Ark arrived in Jerusalem David *"distributed among all the people, among the whole multitude of Israel, both the women and the men, to everyone a loaf of bread, a piece of meat, and a cake of raisins"* (see 2 Samuel 6:1-19).

The significance of this story is both timely and relevant to what is going on in the church today: Eating represents active participation (see John 4:34). The people have a heart to work for God and He wants everyone, male and female, young and old, actively working in His vineyard. If the existing leadership wants to stay ahead of the curve they must understand and conform to the new order and start equipping the saints for the work of the ministry (see Ephesians 4:12,16). It's time for the leaders to train the people and entrust them with their share of the Lord's work. As Jesus said when He was still just a young boy, we must all be about the Master's business.

## Three Reformations

The first reformation, which was a reformation of *doctrine*, was begun in 1517 through Martin Luther's efforts to reform the Catholic Church. Luther's most important contribution to Christianity was that he restored the doctrine of *justification by faith*. In effect, he gave the church back to Jesus and Jesus back to the church. He restored the Son of God as Savior of the world instead of the church substituting itself (or even Mary) as the world's savior.

The second was a reformation of *spirituality*, which was initiated by Charles Parham in 1901 when he began preaching the baptism of the Holy Spirit with the initial evidence of speaking in other tongues. Parham's primary contribution was to restore the ministry of the third member of the Trinity back to Christianity, which the church had completely lost, and in some dominations even denied!

The third will be a reformation of *structure*, which is primarily formed by an organization's government. This last reformation is to restore the presence and ministry of the Father, in all His power and glory, to the church! This reformation will bring the church to the end of its "three day journey" that God has purposed from the beginning of creation, and it may turn out to be the messiest reformation of them all! Nevertheless, a change in church government is absolutely necessary before the church can ascend to the next level of glory that God has prepared for her.

True, apostolic government liberates the people and motivates them to get involved in the Lord's work, while at the same time providing oversight and accountability. Liberty without oversight spawns either laxity or anarchy, depending upon the temperament of the people involved. Responsibility without authority to do what one is responsible for produces frustration and ultimately, rebellion. Neither extreme is acceptable.

So, although cell groups aren't the next move of God, they are scripturally supported and one of the more practical ways to help usher in the next move. They are a vehicle that God can use to transport us to where He wants us to go, though not the only vehicle that He has available. Because cell groups reach into every area of the community they are conducted in, they are a logical and practical means of obeying Christ's command to *"Go therefore and make disciples of all the nations, baptizing them in the name of the Father and of the Son and of the Holy Spirit, teaching them to observe all things that I have commanded you; and lo, I am with you always, even to the end of the age"* (Matthew 28:19-20).

## Apostolic Government

There are several misconceptions that presently exist in the church that we need to examine concerning apostolic government. The most common is the idea that anyone sent is an apostle, because the word "apostle" is derived from the Greek word *apostello*, which means "a sent one." Apostles are indeed sent, but this narrow definition is misleading because *apostello* is also used in Scripture for many who weren't apostles, including the murderers Herod sent to slay the babies in Bethlehem! (see Matthew 2:16). It is also used of John the Baptist, who Jesus specifically called a prophet (see Matthew 11:9-10). So what, or who, are apostles?

Apostles are men ordained of God to establish the church upon the one and only foundation, Jesus Christ! They are commissioned to represent the foundational aspects of Christ's ministry—which they identify with so intimately that they are actually considered an integral part of the foundation! In Paul's epistle to the Ephesians he said that God's house is *"built upon the foundation of the apostles and prophets, Jesus Christ himself being the chief corner stone"* (Ephesians 2:19-20).

True, apostolic government is characterized by its spirit. Anything other than the Spirit of Christ is unacceptable. Jesus was (and is) a man of steel and velvet. He was very stern with

# The Church Triumphant

hypocritical, self-righteous religious leaders but gentle and compassionate with sinners and broken people. He was Lord of all, yet servant of many. He told His disciples, *"You know that those who are considered rulers over the Gentiles lord it over them, and their great ones exercise authority over them. Yet it shall not be so among you; but whoever desires to become great among you shall be your servant. And whoever of you desires to be first shall be slave of all"* (Mark 10:42-44).

Many believe that apostles are supposed to rule over the churches, much as pastors rule their congregations (by operating in both natural and spiritual authority) but as you can see from Christ's admonition above, nothing could be further from the truth. True apostles don't minister by natural authority, which is political (political authority is authority and influence obtained by position), rather, as we discussed in Chapter Three, their authority is spiritual.

Apostles lead by their example. They are the *"first partakers of the fruits!"* (2 Timothy 2:6). Paul said: *"Be ye followers of me, even as I also am of Christ"* (1 Corinthians 11:1, KJV). By going before the brethren, they show the way and serve as examples: Paul exhorted the apostle Timothy to *"be an example to the believers in word, in conduct, in love, in spirit, in faith [and] in purity"* (1 Timothy 4:12).

The Scriptures reveal there are three branches of proper church government; judicial, legislative and executive, which is further divided into natural and spiritual authority. Apostles serve in the judicial realm, operating in spiritual authority. They are authorities in the Logos (as prophets are in the rhema), so they also minister in the legislative branch. For this reason, they were intrusted with the task of writing most of the Scriptures.

# The Church Triumphant

Pastors and elders minister in the executive branch of church government, exercising both natural and spiritual authority. Both pastors and elders are responsible to embrace the vision and teach the doctrine established by the apostles. For those who stumble at this observation, notice that the early church *"continued steadfastly in the apostles' doctrine,"* not the *pastor's* doctrine (see Acts 2:42). To paraphrase David, *"The Lord gave the word [to the apostles]: great was the company of those that published it"* (Psalm 68:11).

Biblically based, true apostolic government will restore evangelistic zeal, *koinonia* (true fellowship) and body ministry (everyone involved in ministry) to the church by both teaching and modeling these three aspects of ministry before the people. True apostles demonstrate the will of God. As Jesus did, they *"both do and teach,"* not just teach (see Acts 1:1).

Another rather common misconception is that apostles are "church planters." Although some apostles do start churches, that is not the defining mark of their ministry. In the same way that some who are sent aren't apostles, many who start churches aren't apostles, either. Instead, apostles are commissioned by the Holy Spirit to *establish* the churches upon the foundation of Christ and His teachings, regardless of who starts them! Paul told the Romans, *"For I long to see you, that I may impart to you some spiritual gift, so that you may be established"* (Romans 1:11). The Greek word *sterizo*, translated *established* means *"to set fast, [to] turn resolutely in a certain direction"* (Strong's 4741).

True, apostolic ministry establishes the churches, providing stability and direction in both doctrine and conduct. First, apostles establish the churches by placing them upon a firm doctrinal foundation. They are responsible to both teach and maintain sound doctrine in the churches they oversee.

# The Church Triumphant

The Bible says the early church *"continued steadfastly in the apostles' doctrine"* (Acts 2:42), and Paul exhorted Timothy to *"Hold fast the form of sound words, which thou hast heard of me... and the things that thou hast heard of me among many witnesses, the same commit thou to faithful men, who shall be able to teach others also"* (2 Timothy 1:13, 2:2). Timothy, Paul's spiritual son, was a second generation apostle. Paul expected Timothy to guard the truth he had received from him and to pass it on to others who would also be faithful to preserve and teach it.

Likewise, when certain men from Jerusalem began corrupting the gospel by teaching the Galatians that they had to keep the law of Moses to be saved, Paul and Barnabas wasted no time and spared no expense in correcting their heretical teachings (see Acts 15:1-2). Besides doctrinal purity, apostles are responsible for the churches spiritual purity as well. In fact, to promote and maintain proper order and unity in the church, apostles are delegated authority in five, specific realms:

1. Authority to establish Doctrine
2. Authority to establish Church Government
3. Authority to Judge and Execute Judgment
4. Authority and Power over all Demons
5. Authority over the Passions of the Flesh

Although restoring apostolic ministry to its proper place in church government is necessary, apostolic ministry, alone, isn't enough. All of the ministerial offices and spiritual gifts must be in operation, functioning together before we will have proper, Bible-based, biblically sound, church government. As mentioned previously, Paul acknowledged the importance of the Holy Spirit's role in establishing the churches in Romans 1:11. Both

# The Church Triumphant

Peter and Paul ministered the baptism of the Holy Spirit through the laying on of hands and gave specific instructions for the proper use of spiritual gifts in their follow-up letters to the churches (see Acts 8:17, 19:6; 1 Corinthians, chapters 12 & 14 and 1 Peter 4:10-11).

Although he was never called one, Moses ministered in the role of an apostle to the nation of Israel (the word apostle isn't found in the Old Testament because it is derived from the Greek word *apostolos*— Strong's 652). When Moses was overwhelmed with the grievous burden of trying to shepherd so many high-maintenance, murmuring and complaining people, he cried out to God,

> *I am not able to bear all these people alone, because the burden is too heavy for me... So the LORD said to Moses: 'Gather to Me seventy men of the elders of Israel, whom you know to be the elders of the people and officers over them; bring them to the tabernacle of meeting, that they may stand there with you. Then I will come down and talk with you there. I will take of the Spirit that is upon you and will put the same upon them; and they shall bear the burden of the people with you, that you may not bear it yourself alone'* (Numbers 11:14,16-17)

Although this is seldom taught in conjunction with the teaching of the nine spiritual gifts, the gift of prophecy is more than just an anointing to enable church members to minister personal words of encouragement and direction to individuals. It is the primary gift that prophets and seers use that enables them to be watchmen (see Ezekiel 3:17). They are eyes and ears to the Body of Christ. Their ministry was meant to assist and complement the apostles' ministry from the very beginning. In the Old Testament they ministered and governed right along-side the kings and in the New Testament, alongside the apostles (see 2 Chronicles 20:14-20, 25:25; Acts 15:25-32).

Besides implementing and maintaining sound doctrine in the early church, the apostles also watched over the flocks to protect them from deceitful shepherds preaching false doctrines and imparting counterfeit spirits! Paul said,

> *But I fear, lest somehow, as the serpent deceived Eve by his craftiness, so your minds may be corrupted from the simplicity that is in Christ. For if he who comes preaches another Jesus whom we have not preached, or if you receive a different spirit which you have not received, or a different gospel which you have not accepted — you may well put up with it!* (2 Corinthians 11:3-4)

Today's church needs apostolic oversight as much, if not even more, than the early church needed it. One important reason is the fact that although many Christians do not believe they can *"receive another spirit, which [they] have not received"*, the truth is, many already have!

Besides establishing the churches by placing them upon a solid doctrinal foundation and by ministering the Spirit and the Spirit's many, precious gifts to the members, there are two more aspects of apostolic ministry that we need to address — implementing local church government offices, then appointing elders to fill those offices, and ministering God's judgment to the Body of Christ.

Apostles establish churches by training, ordaining and overseeing elders in every church they are responsible for. Luke records an interesting account revealing some of the intricacies of this aspect of apostolic ministry in Acts, where immediately

# The Church Triumphant

after Paul was stoned and revived from the dead, he and Barnabas continued on their way,

> *And when they had preached the gospel to that city [Derbe] and made many disciples, they returned to Lystra, Iconium, and Antioch, **strengthening** the souls of the disciples, exhorting them to continue in the faith, and saying, 'We must through many tribulations enter the kingdom of God.' **So when they had appointed elders in every church**, and prayed with fasting, they commended them to the Lord...* (Acts 14:21-23)

The Greek word *episterizo,* translated *strengthening* in this scripture, means to *re-establish* (Strong's 1991). Notice the close proximity of this word to ordaining the elders, and also notice that *elders* here is plural, not singular. There were no New Testament churches ruled by a single pastor. They were all governed alike—by a group of elders.

This is not to say or imply that there were no pastors in the New Testament churches—although Acts and the epistles clearly show that all elders were considered pastors in the early church, they also show that James was considered the leading pastor (or senior elder) of the Jerusalem church (see Acts 12:17, 15:13, 21:18; Galatians 2:12). Likewise, Peter, besides being an apostle, called himself an elder and equated the elders' ministry with shepherding the flock (see 1 Peter 5:1-4).

Although some think that once elders were installed, the apostles who ordained them became subject to them, the Scriptures in no way bear this out. Instead, the Bible shows that the elders willingly submitted themselves to the apostles who appointed them. In fact, Timothy, an apostle who worked alongside Paul, was even instructed to publicly rebuke any elder who sinned! (see Timothy 5:20). The elders had to meet certain qualifications before they were ordained and placed into an office, and then they were required to maintain those qualifications while serving in that office. Paul told the apostle Titus that he left him in Crete to, *"...set in order the things that are lacking, and appoint elders in every city as I commanded you—if a man is blameless, the husband of one wife, having faithful children not accused of dissipation or insubordination. For a bishop must be blameless, as a steward of God, not self-willed, not quick-tempered, not given to wine, not violent, not greedy for money, but hospitable, a lover of what is good, sober-minded, just, holy, self-controlled, holding fast the faithful word as he has been taught..."* (Titus 1:5-9). These qualifications are still applicable today, though admittedly, it is hard to find very many men who can actually satisfy them!

As you can see from the verses above, apostles also have the authority to enforce order in the churches they oversee. Paul threatened the wayward Corinthians with, *"For the kingdom of God is not in word but in power. What do you want? Shall I come to you with a rod, or in love and a spirit of gentleness?* (1 Corinthians 4:20-21), and he meant what he said. In his follow up letter, he wrote, *"Let such a [disobedient] person consider this, that what we are in word by letters when we are absent, such we will also be in deed when we are present"* (2 Corinthians 10:11).

Apostolic authority isn't something to play around with. Paul blinded Barjesus and Peter put Ananias and Sapphira in the grave. Likewise Moses pronounced judgment upon Korah and his household and the earth opened its mouth gulped them down (see Acts 13:6-12, 5:1-11; Numbers 16:28-33). Although the Lord's doctrine of immediate judgment hasn't been preached or demonstrated in the modern, self-centered, lukewarm *"church of the Laodiceans"*, it is one of the many manifestations of the baptism of Fire, so be forewarned! Jesus isn't returning until everything the church has ever had, or has supposed to have had, is fully restored, and the process of restoration is steadily, progressively unfolding before our very eyes. The truth is marching on! (see Revelation 3:14; Acts 3:21).

*The LORD shall send the rod of Your strength out of Zion. Rule in the midst of Your enemies!* (Psalm 110:2)

# Chapter Five
# Christ the Judge

*For the Father judges no one, but has committed all judgment to the Son, ...For as the Father has life in Himself, so He has granted the Son to have life in Himself, and has given Him authority to execute judgment also, because He is the Son of Man* (John 5:22,26-27)

*Let us hear the conclusion of the whole matter: Fear God and keep His commandments, For this is man's all. For God will bring every work into judgment, Including every secret thing, Whether good or evil* (Ecclesiastes 12:13-14)

The Lord is the supreme Judge of all the earth. As Solomon said in the verse quoted above, on a specific, preappointed day He will bring every work into judgment, the good, the bad and the ugly! But before He does, He must first bring the world into accountability, and this is where we come into the picture. But first, before we can be part of that very important, ongoing process, we must learn to judge ourselves correctly because, as Peter said in the following verse, it all begins with us: *"For the time has come for judgment to begin at the house of God; and if it begins with us first, what will be the end of those who do not obey the gospel of God?"* (1 Peter 4:17)

Likewise, Paul tells us that we must judge ourselves by examining ourselves from within if we don't want to be judged from without and chastened for our trespasses: *"For if we would judge ourselves, we would not be judged. But when we are judged, we are chastened by the Lord, that we may not be condemned with the world"* (see 1 Corinthians 11:28, 31-32).

It is easy to see that we need to judge ourselves, but what about the restraints on judging others that Jesus spoke of when He said, *"Judge not that you be not judged"*? (Matthew 7:1). Did He mean it the way it sounds, or is there something deeper going on here? There obviously is because He also said, *"Judge not according to the appearance, but judge righteous judgment"* (John 7:24). At first glance, He seems to be contradicting Himself, but not when these statements are taken in their proper context.

In the Sermon on the Mount (Matthew 5:1-7:29), before Jesus warned us not to judge others, He cautioned those who were listening not to pray as hypocrites pray, nor fast as they do, nor give to be seen of men as hypocrites do—so the context reveals that He is warning them not to judge others with self-righteous judgment as the hypocrites do—but rather to judge both themselves and others with righteous judgment.

Paul gave similar instructions to the Corinthians. He also starts out telling them not to judge but then seems to contradict himself much as Jesus did,

> *But with me it is a very small thing that I should be judged by you or by a human court. In fact, I do not even judge myself. For I know nothing against myself, yet I am not justified by this; but He who judges me is the Lord. **Therefore judge nothing before the time, until the Lord comes**, who will both bring to light the hidden things of darkness and reveal the counsels of the hearts. Then each one's praise will come from God* (1 Corinthians 4:3-5)

Once again we have to look very carefully at the context or we will misinterpret what the apostle is actually telling us not to do. Otherwise, he violated his own instructions, because he then went on to tell them that, even though he wasn't even present, he had already judged a man who was in their congregation who was committing incest! He said, *"For I indeed, as absent in body but present in spirit, have already judged (as though I were present) him who has so done this deed"* (1 Corinthians 5:3).

And if that wasn't enough, he also reproved them for going to civil court before worldly judges instead of appointing someone from their own congregation to arbitrate their disagreements. As Jethro counseled Moses to do many centuries before, they needed to appoint elders to judge and arbitrate the personal disagreements that arose between themselves (see 1 Corinthians 6:1-6; Exodus 18:19-22).

So, what did Paul really mean when he said not to judge anyone before judgment day? Paul is warning them not to judge the motive of another person's heart! We aren't even qualified to judge our own motives, much less someone else's. As Jeremiah observed, *"The heart is deceitful above all things, And desperately wicked; Who can know it?"* (Jeremiah 17:9). And deceitful it is! That is the reason Paul said that although he wasn't conscious of any wrongdoing in his own life, he still didn't judge himself to be completely innocent. Only God is qualified to do that, and *will* do that on judgment day. As Paul said, at that time Christ *"will both bring to light the hidden things of darkness and reveal the [secret] counsels of the hearts"*.

Although we are forbidden to judge another person's motives, we *are* supposed to judge one another's deeds and actions. For instance, Jesus said that we would know false prophets by the fruits of their ministry. If they minister out of love for God and for those they are ministering to, the fruits of their ministry will testify of their sincerity. But if they are ministering for personal fame and gain, the harm done to those they are deceiving will eventually come to light and expose them for who they really are.

This is where we come into the picture. Although judgment *begins* with us, it doesn't end there! Paul said once we've properly judged ourselves and got things straight with God, we are the instruments that He desires to use to punish the disobedient,

> *For the weapons of our warfare are not carnal but mighty in God for pulling down strongholds, casting down arguments and every high thing that exalts itself against the knowledge of God, bringing every thought into captivity to the obedience of Christ, and **being ready to punish all disobedience when your obedience is fulfilled*** (2 Corinthians 10:4-6)

In the past, we have not fully grasped all that God has determined to do through the church. Concerning our conduct in the world, Paul said, *"To the one we are the aroma of death leading to death, and to the other the aroma of life leading to life"* (2 Corinthians 2:16). Although we are glad to be *"the aroma of life leading to life"*, we abhor the idea of being *"the aroma of death leading to death"*. Death has an offensive stench! Nevertheless, before Jesus returns, He has to let the world know what is in store for them if they don't repent. To do that, He has to openly manifest His judgments here on the earth.

Isaiah said something extremely important about this subject that we should consider. It is an eyeopener!

> *With my soul I have desired You in the night, Yes, by my spirit within me I will seek You early; For when Your judgments are in*

# The Church Triumphant

*the earth, The inhabitants of the world will learn righteousness. Let grace be shown to the wicked, Yet he will not learn righteousness; In the land of uprightness he will deal unjustly, And will not behold the majesty of the LORD"* (Isaiah 26:9-10).

We've got to change the way we think about who we are supposed to *"show grace"* to. For example, if we mistakenly treat Gay people as brothers and sisters in the Lord just because they proclaim to be Christians, we justify them in their sin and they have no reason to repent and learn righteousness. Also, if we don't live in such a way that it brings conviction upon them, they cannot be held accountable before God on judgment day. A prime example is Lot. Although Lot is often scorned for choosing to live in Sodom, the wisdom of God had him there for a purpose.

When two angels disguised as men came to execute God's judgment upon Sodom, Lot offered them shelter for the night. When the wicked residents discovered their presence they tried to force Lot to surrender these men over to them so that they might *know* them (that is, to have illicit sexual relations with them). When Lot refused their demands, they realized that Lot's presence was their undoing: *"...they said, 'This one came in to stay here, and he keeps acting as a judge'."* (Genesis 19:9).

They tried to force Lot to compromise because his life testified against them. They unconsciously knew that if Lot could live righteously in that generation, so could they. That is the reason the Gay community is so adamant about the church accepting their perverse lifestyle in this generation. If it doesn't, they are accountable for their sinful deeds. If we do compromise, *we* will be held accountable! Jesus said, *"If I had not come and spoken to them, they would have no sin, but now they have no excuse for their sin... If I had not done among them the works which no one else did, they would have no sin; but now they have seen and also hated both Me and My Father"* (John 15:22,24).

Isaiah said that if we show grace to the wicked, they will not learn righteousness. Why should they? If they believe they won't be condemned when they stand before God, why not go ahead and fulfill their lustful passions? Many Christians are confused about what their proper stance concerning this matter should be, but the Scriptures could not be more clear and direct: *"Do you not know that the unrighteous will not inherit the kingdom of God? Do not be deceived. Neither fornicators, nor idolaters, nor adulterers, nor homosexuals, nor sodomites"* (1 Corinthians 6:9).

This warning against deception is both timeless and timely. It applies to all ages but it is especially important for this generation. It clearly shows that God has not changed His mind about the sin of homosexuality — *"You shall not lie with a male as with a woman. It is an abomination"* (Leviticus 18:22). Our cultural norms do not change God's eternal standards of truth and righteousness. The cross of Christ does not make this sin, which was an abomination under the Old Covenant, acceptable under the New. *Forgivable* upon repentance, *yes! Acceptable* under any circumstances, definitely *not!*

Why is this particular sin such a serious matter? Because once a society accepts homosexuality and embraces it as an alternate lifestyle, it has reached *the fullness of iniquity* and is subject to God's wrath. Paul prefaced his discourse to the Romans on homosexuality with this solemn warning, *"For the wrath of God is revealed from heaven against all ungodliness and unrighteousness of men, who suppress the truth in unrighteousness"* (Romans 1:18).

# The Church Triumphant

There is a distinct difference between chastisement and wrath. God chastens those He loves to bring them to repentance but He utterly destroys those who willfully sin and stubbornly refuse to repent. Proverbs promises, *"He who is often rebuked, and hardens his neck, Will suddenly be destroyed, and that without remedy"* (Proverbs 29:1).

As this scripture implies, God doesn't hastily destroy anyone. Before He does, He usually gives them ample time to repent (see Revelation 2:21), but some people mistake His patience for His approval of their misdeeds! Solomon said, *"Because the sentence against an evil work is not executed speedily, therefore the heart of the sons of men is fully set in them to do evil"* (Ecclesiastes 8:11).

God is compassionate and longsuffering. As long as there is hope of redemption, He waits patiently, giving people plenty of time to repent. But once a nation reaches the fullness of iniquity and there is no longer any hope of redemption, the only recourse God has left is to destroy that nation. David said, *"The LORD is known by the judgment He executes; The wicked is snared in the work of his own hands... The wicked shall be turned into hell, And all the nations that forget God"* (Psalm 9:16-17).

How do we know when a society has reached the point of no return? One of the primary indicators is unrestrained, unashamed, homosexual behavior. When someone's sinful deeds are exposed and brought to light, if instead of being ashamed that person hardens their heart and *"glories in their shame"*, there is little, if any, hope of redemption. Paul called these people *enemies of the cross,*

*For many walk, of whom I have told you often, and now tell you even weeping, that they are the enemies of the cross of Christ:*

*whose end is destruction, whose god is their belly, and **whose glory is in their shame**—who set their mind on earthly things* (Philippians 3:18)

This is exactly what we see taking place in our nation when homosexuals and lesbians unashamedly march hand–in–hand down our city streets in *Gay Pride Parades!*

God has erected a fourfold border wall to restrain iniquity. The first barrier against sin is man's conscience. But when individuals defile and sear their conscience and willingly, even pridefully, behave shamefully, this wall is breached. The next boundary that God has placed in the path of the wicked is the collective conscience of the populous, usually manifested in the form of societal taboos.

For example, in America, a few decades ago, if a girl became pregnant out of wedlock she was ashamed and tried to hide her sin from the public. Now we have television shows titled, *"16 and Pregnant"*! Likewise, in the past Gay people kept their sin a secret. Now they *come out of the closet* and publicly flaunt their shameful conduct, and instead of the public condemning them, *they celebrate them!* They are like the immoral Corinthians that Paul rebuked, *"And you are puffed up, and have not rather mourned, that he who has done this deed might be taken away from among you"* (1 Corinthians 5:2). Hollywood has capitalized on this insanity by flooding the public airways and theaters with homosexual shows and movies.

If society not only accepts this perversion but even takes pleasure in it, God can no longer use the collective consciousness of society to bring correction. A society that accepts homosexuality as the norm has to first reject God! Paul said this is actually the reason they are subject to God's wrath,

# The Church Triumphant

*And even as they did not like to retain God in their knowledge, God gave them over to a reprobate mind, to do those things which are not convenient; Being filled with all unrighteousness, fornication... haters of God, despiteful, proud... without natural affection... Who knowing the judgment of God, that they which commit such things are worthy of death, not only do the same, but have pleasure in them that do them* (Romans 1:28-29, 32, KJV)

God treats us the way we treat Him. If we reject Him, invariably, He will reject us because of the immutable law of sowing and reaping—we always reap what we sow.

The third restraint God ordained to curb iniquity is civil law. In the early days of America, even adultery was considered a crime. Sodomy was known as a "crime against nature" (a phrase taken directly from Paul's discourse on homosexuality in Romans 1:26). Almost all of the sodomy laws have been stricken from the books because our lawgivers have forsaken God's standards and replaced them with societies' cultural norms.

This leaves only one restraint left to hold back the present flood of iniquity that is inundating the nation—the church—and the satanic waves of public pressure are pounding upon that dike to the point that it is almost at the breaking point.

One major cause of the rabid advancement of the homosexual agenda in America is fatherless homes and feminism. Homosexuality is one of the many, harmful fruits of the feminist movement that is so prevalent in the world today. Although feminism certainly isn't the only cause of homosexuality, it has played a significant role in the rise of this perversion.

When God reproved Judah for their iniquitous behavior, He accused them of doing the same things that Israel had done before they were carried off by the Assyrians. Through Ezekiel,

# The Church Triumphant

He gave us several important insights revealing the root cause of Sodomy,

> *Indeed everyone who quotes proverbs will use this proverb against you: 'Like mother, like daughter!' You are your mother's daughter, loathing husband and children; and you are the sister of your sisters, who loathed their husbands and children... Look, this was the iniquity of your sister Sodom: She and her daughter had pride, fullness of food, and abundance of idleness; neither did she strengthen the hand of the poor and needy. And they were haughty and committed abomination before Me; therefore I took them away as I saw fit* (Ezekiel 16:44-45, 49-50)

Why does rejecting God and God ordained authority ultimately result in homosexuality? Because we are created in God's image, *"So God created man in His own image; in the image of God He created him; male and female He created them"* (Genesis 1:27). **To reject God is to reject one's own image!** When a society embraces evolution as their source and ceases to exalt God and acknowledge Him as their creator, they lose the only infallible standard that exists by which right and wrong may be measured —good becomes evil and evil is esteemed as good—male becomes female and female becomes male. When they deny God His rightful place in their minds they become confused in their identity and they no longer see themselves as who and what they really are.

When men and women reverse their proper roles and men submit to their wives instead of living according to God's pattern, they bring confusion into the home. When Adam disobeyed God and instead obeyed Eve, Satan gained control.

# The Church Triumphant

When husbands repeat Adam's sin, Satan reigns in that family and perverts those whom he gains dominion over.

When women reject God's word and strive for equality (or even supremacy) instead of honoring their fathers and respecting their husbands as they should, they reject God. God and His word are one. You cannot reject one without rejecting the other. When women respect their husbands and men honor their wives as God said they should, they are blessed. Conversely, when men are abusive or neglectful toward their wives and wives despise their husbands and refuse to respect them, they sabotage their own marriages and inevitably reap the due rewards of their deeds.

When parents fail to abide by God's instructions concerning their proper roles in their relationship, they bring confusion into their homes. As a result, their children also become confused in their identity and proper roles. When men submit to their wives instead of their wives submitting to them and women rule over their husbands instead of obeying them as God commanded them to do, inevitably, the results are catastrophic.

Christian women who think that husbands and wives are supposed to be considered equal should pay close attention to what Peter commanded husbands to do: *"Husbands, likewise, dwell with them with understanding, giving honor to the wife, as to the weaker vessel, and as being heirs together of the grace of life, that your prayers may not be hindered"* (1 Peter 3:7). God's word is clear. There should be no confusion as to what their proper roles should be,

*Wives, submit to your own husbands, as to the Lord. For the husband is head of the wife, as also Christ is head of the church; and He is the Savior of the body. Therefore, just as the church is*

*subject to Christ, so let the wives be to their own husbands in everything. Husbands, love your wives, just as Christ also loved the church and gave Himself for her... This is a great mystery, but I speak concerning Christ and the church. Nevertheless let each one of you in particular so love his own wife as himself, and let the wife see that she respects her husband* (Ephesians 5:22-25, 32-33)

Thus we can see that the fullness of the cup of iniquity is measured by the level of homosexuality that is prevalent in society. It is virtually a barometer that reveals the level of rejection and animosity that any given society has toward their Creator. For instance, in this nation, besides authorizing the slaughter of unborn children, America's Supreme Court Justices have forbidden our children to pray in school and many of the schools even forbid the students mentioning the name of Jesus, reading their Bibles or quoting scripture in public speeches. The federal judges have forbidden the display of the Ten Command-ments in court houses and even the display of Nativity Scenes on public squares. Yet God has blessed this nation far above and beyond every other nation on the earth! The magnitude of her ingratitude reaches high into the heavens!

Many of those who are in government have departed from God's laws and conspired to *"cast away their cords [of restraint] from us."* Therefore, since *"they did not like to retain God in their knowledge, God gave them over to a debased mind, to do those things which are not fitting"* (see Psalm 2:1-3 and Romans 1:28). There is a day of reckoning coming! As Peter said concerning those who teach heretical doctrines and deceive the people, *"...their judgment has not been idle, and their destruction does not slumber"* (2 Peter 2:3).

# The Church Triumphant

When homosexuality is not only tolerated and accepted by the church, but actually approved of as an "alternate lifestyle" (as in recognizing homosexuals and lesbians as saved—instead of as sinners in need of salvation—performing same-sex marriages and ordaining homosexual and lesbian pastors and priests in churches), the last barrier erected to restrain iniquity is breached and the cup of iniquity is full and running over! When this takes place God's only recourse is to destroy that nation. One can see that America has already reached a very dangerous level of depravity and neither her federal judges nor the church is doing anything to alter her downward spiral toward destruction!

When God advised Abraham that his descendants had to wait four hundred years before they could invade Canaan, it was for this very reason—the Canaanite people had not yet reached the fullness of iniquity. God explained to Abraham that the reason for the delay was *"the iniquity of the Amorites is not yet full"* (see Genesis 15:13-16, KJV).

Many have wondered why God told Moses that Israel was to kill everything that breathed when they invaded Canaan. Although Moses was commanded to offer peace to those who were in the lands that he was to pass through on the way to Canaan—*"But of the cities of these peoples which the LORD your God gives you as an inheritance, you shall let nothing that breathes remain alive"* (Deuteronomy 20:16)—it was because once an entire society reaches the final stages of iniquitous behavior, there is no redemption possible. As in the law of seeds, they can only reproduce after their own kind. Jesus said, *"For a good tree does not bear bad fruit, nor does a bad tree bear good fruit"* (Luke 6:43).

The presence of unrestrained homosexual activity isn't the only manifestation of the fullness of iniquity. Hostility toward the righteous is another. In his epistle to the Thessalonians Paul accused the Jews of killing the Lord Jesus and persecuting their own prophets. He said the Jews were *"contrary to all men: Forbidding us to speak to the Gentiles that they might be saved, to fill up their sins always: for the wrath [of God] is come upon them to the uttermost"* (see 1 Thessalonians 2:14-16). Paul not only experienced their malicious hatred, but he prophesied that in the perilous times that we are now in, that we would experience it too. Every sign that Paul gave us is rampant in America today,

> *But know this, that in the last days perilous times will come: For men will be lovers of themselves, lovers of money, boasters, proud, blasphemers, disobedient to parents, un-thankful, unholy, unloving, unforgiving, slanderers, without self- control, brutal, despisers of good* (2 Timothy 3:3)

The Greek word *aphilagathos*, which is translated *despisers of good* in this text literally means *hostile to virtue* (Strong's 865). This hostility is directed toward anyone and everyone who dares to oppose their wicked lifestyle and condone righteous living. As Isaiah said, *"The way of peace they have not known, And there is no justice in their ways; They have made themselves crooked paths... [and] he who departs from evil makes himself a prey"* (Isaiah 59:8,15). When we refuse to compromise and agree with them we bring condemnation upon them and this invokes hatred toward us.

For those who wonder why America hasn't already been destroyed, take note that God's judgments operate on successive, ascending levels of severity (see Leviticus 26:14-39; Ezekiel 14:12-21). On a national level—if, after repeatedly warning the people they still refuse to repent—He often starts out with severe droughts and uncontrollable wildfires in some parts of the country while raging storms accompanied by devastating floods wreck havoc in other areas. This is often coupled with economic troubles and recessions that afflict the whole nation. If that doesn't produce the desired results, He escalates His chastisements with calamities such as pestilence, famines, violent earthquakes, mob violence from within and if that still doesn't bring the people to repentance, as a last resort He sends the sword of war from without. Many of these judgments have been rampant on American soil since the beginning of this millennium. God isn't ignoring our sinful conduct. The King of kings is faithful to His word. He will not sit idly by and watch while Satan steals His heritage!

On a personal level, a clear example of the process of God's chastisement is shown in Paul's writings. He teaches us that if we take communion unworthily without first examining ourselves and repenting so that we can partake of it with a clear, undefiled conscience, we are subjected to a successive, ascending, three level chastisement program. Paul instructed the Corinthians to examine themselves before taking communion and to be respectful of one another while taking it, *"For he who eats and drinks in an unworthy manner eats and drinks judgment to himself, not discerning the Lord's body. For this reason many are weak and sick among you, and many sleep"* (see 1 Corinthians 11:28-32).

*Weakness–sickness–death!* And notice that Paul said *many* are suffering from God's chastisements. It should also be noted that since all of God's ways are equal, if one takes communion worthily there is a wonderful, threefold blessing to be enjoyed as well — strength and vitality; healing and health; and life more abundant!

## Imprecatory Prayer

Besides judging and executing judgment in the world through our personal lifestyle and testimony, we are also authorized to execute judgment though imprecatory prayer. Wikipedia defines imprecatory prayer as prayers *"that invoke judgment, calamity, or curses, upon one's enemies or those perceived as the enemies of God."*

Two such examples of this type of prayer are found in Psalm 69 and Psalm109. Although Psalm 109 is too long to quote here, it is perhaps the severest prayer in the entire Bible. It is directed toward those who slander others and reward evil for good, and interestingly enough, when you read it take note that David, who was *"a man after God's own heart"*, is the one who prayed this prayer! God doesn't always think like we think He thinks! One Psalmists exclaimed, *"O LORD, how great are Your works! Your thoughts are very deep. A senseless man does not` know, Nor does a fool understand this"* (Psalm 92:5-6).

Various models and examples of imprecatory prayers, to one degree of severity or another, are found in Psalm 5, 6, 11, 35, 37, 40, 52, 54, 56, 58, 79, 83, 137, 143 and James 5:17-18. Although we will cover this type of prayer more fully in the chapter on prayer strategies, we need to examine two more of these prayers while we are on this subject.

The first is Psalm 35, because this one gives us an example of both defensive and offensive prayer (I've divided this prayer into two paragraphs for clarity). As you read this prayer, notice that David shifted from pleading for help in the first paragraph to decreeing his enemies defeat in the second. He first asked God to defend and protect him from his enemies' vicious attacks then he began decreeing their destruction. He went from being defensive to being offensive and declared, *let* the angel pursue, overtake and punish his antagonists (verses 4-8),

*Plead my cause, O LORD, with those who strive with me; Fight against those who fight against me. Take hold of shield and buckler, And stand up for my help. Also draw out the spear, And stop those who pursue me. Say to my soul, 'I am your salvation.'*

*Let those be put to shame and brought to dishonor Who seek after my life; Let those be turned back and brought to confusion Who plot my hurt. Let them be like chaff before the wind, And let the angel of the LORD chase them. Let their way be dark and slippery, And let the angel of the LORD pursue them. For without cause they have hidden their net for me in a pit, Which they have dug without cause for my life. Let destruction come upon him unexpectedly, And let his net that he has hidden catch himself; Into that very destruction let him fall. And my soul shall be joyful in the LORD; It shall rejoice in His salvation* (Psalm 35:1-9)

Notice the similarity of this Psalm to Genesis 1. David boldly decreed and commanded his enemies' destruction in much the same way that God commanded light to come into being in the beginning. David's prayers were aggressive, not passive or pleading.

The second imprecatory prayer we need to examine is a prayer that James wrote about in his epistle to the twelve tribes of Israel. He used Elijah praying for God to punish Israel by sending a drought as an example of the effectiveness of a righteous man's prayers. Besides that important point, we should also note that after Israel repented, Elijah prayed for God to release them from His divine judgment and bless them with rain. James said, *"Elijah was a man with a nature like ours, and he prayed earnestly that it would not rain; and it did not rain on the land for three years and six months. And he prayed again, and the heaven gave rain, and the earth produced its fruit"* (James 5:17-18). It is important that we remember to pray for mercy once someone has repented and turned his or her heart toward God. Elijah's prayers first stopped, and later, restored the rain over the land of Israel.

Another important lesson we should learn from this passage of scripture is, as James pointed out, *"Elijah was a man with a nature like ours"*. Although Elijah was certainly a great man of God, Jesus said, *"For I say to you, among those born of women there is not a greater prophet than John the Baptist; but he who is least in the kingdom of God is greater than he"* (Luke 7:28). When it comes to judgment and justice, God is completely impartial. He is no respecter of persons. He is as attentive to your prayers as He was to Elijah's!

Although we should be careful to never ask God to execute a judgment of our own upon anyone, we *should* pray for Him, at the appropriate times, to execute those judgments that *He* has prescribed in His own word (see Isaiah 10:1; Psalm 149:9; Revelation 16:7). Remember, *"when [God's] judgments are in the earth, The inhabitants of the world will learn righteousness. Let grace be shown to the wicked, Yet he will not learn righteousness; In the land of uprightness he will deal unjustly, And will not behold the majesty of the LORD"* (Isaiah 26:9-10).

We are not doing habitual sinners a favor by showing them grace when, besides warning them, we should be doing what Elijah did, asking God to discipline them so that they might learn the fear of the Lord and come to repentance. Jude said, *"And on some have compassion, making a distinction; but others save with fear, pulling them out of the fire, hating even the garment defiled*

# The Church Triumphant

by the flesh" (Jude 1:22-23). Likewise, Peter said, "*The Lord is not slack concerning His promise [of returning and executing fiery judgment upon the wicked], as some count slackness, but is longsuffering... not willing that any should perish but that all should come to repentance*" (see 2 Peter 3:4-9).

There is one more aspect to this subject that we need to address. There are times when the accuser of the brethren accuses us before God and we need to go before the courts of heaven and defend ourselves. Isaiah said, "*Put Me in remembrance; Let us contend together; State your case, that you may be acquitted*" (Isaiah 43:26). We should remember that Satan often accuses us through our own brethren, sometimes even through those in our own household! It is a mistake to simply ignore Satan's accusations, even when you know that everything he is accusing you of is false. God promised that "*No weapon formed against you shall prosper, And every tongue which rises against you in judgment You shall condemn. This is the heritage of the servants of the LORD, And their righteousness is from Me," Says the LORD*" (Isaiah 54:17), but we should never take God's promises for granted. You have to state your case and ask God to vindicate you as Isaiah said to do.

When Jesus was accused falsely, He refused to answer in His own defense or ask His Father to deliver Him, so His enemy prevailed over Him (or so he thought)! Jesus refused to defend Himself both for our sake and so that He could complete His mission, as He told Peter when He rebuked him for attempting to use a sword in His defense: "*But Jesus said to [Peter], 'Put your sword in its place, for all who take the sword will perish by the sword. Or do you think that I cannot now pray to My Father, and He will provide Me with more than twelve legions of angels? How then could the Scriptures be fulfilled...?'.*" (Matthew 26:52-54)

# The Church Triumphant

If Jesus was required to pray for the Father's angelic protection before He could obtain it, even though He had many promises directly relating to His safety, we certainly have to do the same. Regardless of what type of protection or defense we may need—whether from natural calamity and disasters or from an enemies' slanderous accusations—we should and must ask God to shield us on all sides. By stating our case before God's throne and declaring our side of the story when we are accused, we shield ourselves from Satan's malicious attacks and manifest God's righteous judgments in the earth.

*For You, O LORD, will bless the righteous; With favor You will surround him as with a shield* (Psalm 5:12)

# Chapter Six
# Christ the warrior

*The LORD is a man of war; The LORD is His name* (Exodus 15:3).

Although many are not aware that Moses called God a *Man of war*, as in the verse above, nearly every Christian is familiar with Paul's spiritual warfare scripture, *"For though we walk in the flesh, we do not war according to the flesh. For the weapons of our warfare are not carnal but mighty in God for pulling down strongholds"* (2 Corinthians 10:3-4). But one day as I was reading this verse, I impulsively asked, *"Lord, just what are our weapons?"* His instant response startled me. He said, *"promises, prayer, prophecy and praise!"* Four strategic weapons! We will see that when these weapons are used properly, we are not only victorious in pulling down strongholds, we are also awarded the spoils of war!

Since in Scripture seven means complete, before you can call a doctrine complete you have to discover all seven of its precepts. So, as in every other doctrine, the actual process of applying these four weapons involves seven precepts (there are four weapons because four means to *rule* or *dominate*). The progression actually looks like this:

*Promises* (both Logos and Rhema)
Principal (Faith and Patience)
Problem (Opposition—Spiritual Warfare)
*Prayer* (Persevering, Prevailing)

# The Church Triumphant

*Prophecy* (revealing Strategy, Timing and Location)
*Praise* and Worship (Accessing and Releasing Victorious Power)
Provision (Spoils of War)

As we can see from the above list, everything starts with God's abundant, immutable *promises*. And Paul said, *"For all the promises of God in Him are Yes, and in Him Amen, to the glory of God through us"* (2 Corinthians 1:20). Although Paul said the answer to every biblical promise that we ask for is always "yes and amen", there is a divine *principle* that every promise is also conditional, meaning before it will come to pass we must satisfy the conditions that it is predicated upon. What are those conditions? Although some promises may have their own, individual conditions attached to them, two conditions are common to every promise—*faith and patience*. As Hebrews admonishes us, *"do not become sluggish, but imitate those who through faith and patience inherit the promises"* (Hebrews 6:12).

Once we receive a specific promise from God and have accepted His conditions (whether we understand them or not), we immediately encounter a *problem*—Satan is always standing between us and the fulfillment of the promise, and the warfare is always in direct proportion to the magnitude of the promise. Why? Because God receives honor and is glorified every time He fulfills a promise and Satan is envious of God's glory. He tries to block and steal it. Therefore, war isn't optional; it is inevitable (see Hebrews 10:32).

For example, when Moses responded (prematurely) to his calling to deliver Israel from slavery, he came under attack and had to flee to the backside of the desert. Likewise, after Joseph received two dreams promising him that his brothers would one day bow before him, he was promptly sold into slavery and later thrust into prison. His ordeal lasted for a full thirteen years. And when David was chosen to be King Saul's replacement, he immediately came under attack. Demonic forces in Saul sought every means possible to kill David. Even Jesus was driven into the wilderness to war with Satan immediately after His Father anointed Him with the Holy Spirit and audibly declared from heaven that He was His own beloved Son.

Thus we see that every promise brings us into direct confrontation with Satan, and this is where our God given weapons come into play. Paul's admonition to the Ephesians to *"take the **helmet** of salvation"* reveals that the war is a mental, emotional battle, fought primarily in the mind—and it is waged with *"the sword of the Spirit, which is the word [promises] of God"*.

> *Therefore take up the whole armor of God, that you may be able to withstand in the evil day... Stand therefore, having girded your waist with truth, having put on the breastplate of righteousness, and having shod your feet with the preparation of the gospel of peace; above all, taking the shield of faith with which you will be able to quench all the fiery darts of the wicked one. And take the helmet of salvation, and the sword of the Spirit, which is the word of God; praying always with all prayer and supplication in the Spirit, being watchful to this end with all perseverance and supplication for all the saints (Ephesians 6:13-18)*

How do we wield this sword? How is it used in battle? Simply by *"praying always with all prayer and supplication in the Spirit... with all perseverance"* So we see that persevering, prevailing prayer based upon God's promises is the first step toward achieving victory. The second step is hearing God's *prophetic directions*, which involves patiently waiting upon God to show us what to do.

Without God's clear, prophetic directions, which reveal His *strategy* for effective warfare, we are fighting blindly. We are struggling against an opponent who is a master of darkness and deception. We are swinging wildly in hope of connecting with an enemy we cannot even see! Without first knowing God's strategy we are constantly frustrated because we are attempting to fight using our own tactics instead of His.

Besides God's strategy, prophecy gives us both *timing* and *direction*, without which, as we have seen, we are fighting blindly. But once we discern God's clear, precise directions, victory is within our grasp. All that remains is the triumphant expression of our faith—declaring and releasing the power of God's word. Observe what David said as he ran toward Goliath,

> *Then David said to the Philistine, "You come to me with a sword, with a spear, and with a javelin. But I come to you in the name of the LORD of hosts... This day the LORD will deliver you into my hand, and I will strike you and take your head from you... that all the earth may know that there is a God in Israel. Then all this assembly shall know that the LORD does not save with sword and spear; for the battle is the LORD'S* (see 1 Samuel 17:45-47)

David faced impossible odds, yet he still prevailed. Centuries later, King Jehoshaphat and his people were confronted with similar odds when three hostile nations came against Jerusalem. Jehoshaphat took Judah through all seven precepts of warfare, cumulating in a tremendous victory that gave them an abundance of the spoils of war. As we walk through the process, remember the seven precepts, in order, are:

# The Church Triumphant

*Promise* (Logos and Rhema)
Principal (Faith and Patience)
Problems (Opposition — Spiritual Warfare)
*Prayer* (Prevailing, Persistent, Persevering)
*Prophecy* (Strategy, Timing, Location)
*Praise* and Worship (Accessing and Releasing Power)
Provision (Spoils of War)

> *It happened after this that the people of Moab with the people of Ammon, and others... came... against Jehoshaphat... And Jehoshaphat feared, and set himself to seek the LORD, and proclaimed a fast throughout all Judah* (2 Chronicles 20:1-4)

Jehoshaphat realized they were helpless against the combined armies that confronted them, so he went into his armory and pulled out his first weapon — he turned to the Lord in *prayer*. As we can see from the following verses, his prayer was directed by and based upon God's specific, immutable *promises* that He had previously given Israel. Also notice that Jehoshaphat asked God to judge his adversaries as he waited for Him to tell him what to do,

> *Then Jehoshaphat stood... and said: 'O LORD God of our fathers... Are You not our God, who drove out the inhabitants of this land before Your people Israel, and gave it to the descendants of Abraham Your friend forever? And they... have built You a sanctuary in it for Your name, saying, 'If disaster comes upon us — we will... cry out to You in our affliction, and You will hear and save.' And now, here are the people of Ammon, Moab, and Mount Seir — whom You would not let Israel invade when they came out of the land of Egypt... here they are, rewarding us by*

*coming to throw us out of Your possession which You have given us to inherit.* **O our God, will You not judge them?** *For we have no power against this great multitude that is coming against us; nor do we know what to do, but our eyes are upon You'* (2 Chronicles 20:5-12)

God responded by anointing one of the sons of Asaph with a *prophetic* utterance to encourage them and give them timing, location and direction, thus showing them His strategy for success in the upcoming battle,

*Then the Spirit of the LORD came upon Jahaziel... And he said... Thus says the LORD: 'Do not be afraid nor dismayed because of this great multitude, for the battle is not yours, but God's. Tomorrow go down against them... you will find them at the end of the brook before the Wilderness of Jeruel. You will not need to fight in this battle. Position yourselves, stand still and see the salvation of the LORD... Do not fear or be dismayed... for the LORD is with you'* (2 Chronicles 20:14:17)

Once Jehoshaphat heard these instructions, he set about obeying them to the letter. In the process, he uttered one of the most important exhortations concerning prophetic ministry found in Scripture,

*...as they went out, Jehoshaphat stood and said, 'Hear me, O Judah and you inhabitants of Jerusalem: Believe in the LORD your God, and you shall be established; believe His prophets, and you shall prosper'* (2 Chronicles 20:20)

# The Church Triumphant

In spite of the massive army that he could see and hear, Jehoshaphat chose to put his trust in God. His faith and obedience moved God to fight for Judah, as He had promised in His word. All that was left for them to do was worship and *praise* God as they watched Him work, and then gather in the spoils,

> And when [Jehoshaphat] had consulted with the people, he appointed those who should sing to the LORD, and who should praise the beauty of holiness, as they went out before the army and were saying: 'Praise the LORD, For His mercy endures forever.' Now when they began to sing and to praise, the LORD set ambushes against the people of Ammon, Moab, and Mount Seir, who had come against Judah; and they were defeated. For the people of Ammon and Moab stood up against the inhabitants of Mount Seir to utterly kill and destroy them. And when they had made an end of the inhabitants of Seir, they helped to destroy one another. So when Judah came to a place overlooking the wilderness, they looked toward the multitude; and there were their dead bodies, fallen on the earth. No one had escaped.
>
> When Jehoshaphat and his people came to take away their spoil, they found among them an abundance of valuables on the dead bodies, and precious jewelry, which they stripped off for themselves, more than they could carry away; **and they were three days gathering the spoil** because there was so much (2 Chronicles 20:21-25)

Once God's timing is discerned and His strategies are put into motion through obedience, there's nothing that can stand in our way. As it was with Judah, when in our helplessness we turn to the Lord and completely trust in Him, what the enemy sends for evil God very often turns into a blessing. In Judah's case, a blessing of abundant *provision*! One of God's covenant promises is *"I will divide Him a portion with the great, And He [Jesus] shall divide the spoil with the strong"* (Isaiah 53:12). And who are the strong? Those who, like Abraham, when faced with a seemingly hopeless situation refuse to give up. Instead they hold fast to the promises and choose to believe in the faithfulness of God (see Romans 4:18-20).

We can expect better days ahead. The preaching of the kingdom of God includes the restoration of the apostolic anointing accompanied with the baptism of Fire. This message is bringing *power, purification and **provision*** to the church. As He did in Bible days, Christ is commissioning His chosen apostles with power and authority to rule with Him. He is giving them authority to judge both the church and the world alongside of Himself—and together they are bringing the world into accountability and the church into the mature image of Christ—and in the process, just as He promised He is dividing the spoils of war with the strong. As Solomon said, *"A good man leaves an inheritance to his children's children, But the wealth of the sinner is stored up for the righteous"* (Proverbs 12:22).

# Chapter Seven
# Open Heavens

*Now I saw heaven opened, and behold, a white horse. And He who sat on him was called Faithful and True, and in righteousness He judges and makes war* (Revelation 19:11)

When Philip brought Nathanael to meet the Messiah, Jesus revealed his character through a word of knowledge. When Nathanael, in his amazement at the supernatural nature of Jesus' greeting, asked, *"How do you know me?*, Jesus replied, *"Before Philip called you, when you were under the fig tree, I saw you"*. His instant response was, *"Rabbi, You are the Son of God! You are the King of Israel!"* Jesus's reply to Nathanael's revelation of who He was (and is) is the first mention of open heavens in the New Testament: *"Because I said to you, 'I saw you under the fig tree,' do you believe? You will see greater things than these... Most assuredly, I say to you, hereafter you shall see heaven open, and the angels of God ascending and descending upon the Son of Man"* (see John 1:43-51).

Jesus is the same today as He was then. God's ways never change. Because Nathanael willingly embraced the prophetic ministry of Christ, he was qualified to experience the next thing on His agenda, the opening of the heavens! Many of Christ's followers who have fully embraced the restoration of the prophetic anointing and ministry are already sensing and experiencing the effects of God pulling back the curtains and opening the heavens to them.

But there's more to this mystery than just the church basking in the supernatural outpouring of the Spirit of God. When God opens the heavens to us, there is always a corresponding opening of the fountains within our souls. This kingdom principle is first introduced in Genesis,

> *In the six hundredth year of Noah's life, in the second month, the seventeenth day of the month, on that day all the fountains of the great deep were broken up, and the windows of heaven were opened* (Genesis 7:11)

There's a new move of righteousness coming! When God opens the heavens and shines His glorious light upon us, of necessity, it automatically exposes the deep, hidden darkness lurking within our souls. As Isaiah cried out, *"Rain down, you heavens, from above, And let the skies pour down righteousness; Let the earth open, let them bring forth salvation, And let righteousness spring up together. I, the LORD, have created it"* (Isaiah 45:8).

As we saw above, the first mention of God opening the heavens is in Genesis. Fittingly, the last mention is in Revelation, *"Now I saw heaven opened, and behold, a white horse. And He who sat on him was called Faithful and True, and in righteousness He judges and makes war"* (Revlation19:11). Between these two instances there are many more occurrences, but these two illustrate what the doctrine of Open Heavens is all about—God's inevitable, righteous judgments and intervention in man's affairs, both to reward the righteous for their sacrifice and service and rain destruction and ruin down upon the wicked—the wicked's vain attempts to deny His impending judgments, notwithstanding.

When God opens the heavens, He removes all restrictions between Himself and His people. Our prayers are readily received and responded to (although not always *as* or *when* we think they should). Because of this, there is a brutal preparation and cleansing process that we must go through before we have open access to His unveiled presence and unlimited resources. As Solomon said, *"The spirit of a man is the lamp of the LORD, Searching all the inner depths of his heart"* (Proverbs 20:27).

This thorough cleansing experience is one of the primary works of *"the baptism of Fire"* and is part of God's end-time program for the church. John the Baptist preached and promised both the baptism of the Holy Spirit *and* the baptism of Fire,

> *I indeed baptize you with water; but One mightier than I is coming, whose sandal strap I am not worthy to loose. He will baptize you with the Holy Spirit and fire. His winnowing fan is in His hand, and He will thoroughly clean out His threshing floor, and gather the wheat into His barn; but the chaff He will burn with unquenchable fire* (Luke 3:16-17)

Of the seven baptisms, the baptism of Fire is the only "two–part" baptism. Actually, it is two baptisms in one. It consists of both power and purification because these two are inseparable. As John prophesied in the verses above, God's powerful, fiery presence both completely saves and *throughly* cleanses and purifies.

Isaiah said that before God fully restores Israel to their proper place and relationship with Him, He will have *"washed away the filth of the daughters of Zion, and purged the blood of Jerusalem from her midst, by the spirit of judgment and by the spirit of burning"* (Isaiah 4:4). The, *"spirit of judgment and the spirit of burning"* is the very essence of the baptism of Fire. Right before Jesus went to the Cross, He told His disciples, *"I came to send fire on the earth, and how I wish it were already kindled! But I have a baptism to be baptized with, and how distressed I am till it is accomplished!"* (Luke 12:49-50).

Many are praying for God to restore power to the church, and indeed it is greatly needed. The baptism of Fire is the answer to their prayers. It is next, nay, *now* on God's agenda for the church. Without it, we cannot be prepared, as is necessary, to ascend with Jesus to rule over the darkness of this world as He planned and purposed for us to do from the beginning of creation.

Our pattern is Jesus, Himself. Before He was allowed to ascend into the heavens and assume His seat at the Father's right hand, He had to first descend into the abyss and defeat death, Hell and the grave. Paul asked, *"Now this, 'He ascended'— what does it mean but that He also first descended into the lower parts of the earth? He who descended is also the One who ascended far above all the heavens, that He might fill all things"* (see Ephesians 4:9-10; Revelations 1:18; Hebrews 5:8-9).

We must follow in Christ's footsteps. The greater the promise—the higher the calling—the deeper the depths of despair and agony we are thrust into. This fiery trial is often called, *the dark night of the soul.*

Paul tells us that the things the Israelites experienced *"happened to them as examples, and they were written for our admonition, upon whom the ends of the ages have come"* (1 Corinthians 10:11). The opposition the Patriarchs faced was intense. Jacob had to wrestle with an angel all night and prevail before he was allowed to enter into his promised possession in Canaan. Joseph was betrayed by his own brethren and allowed to "rot in prison", seemingly without hope of ever getting out, to prepare him for greatness. David was pursued by Saul for thirteen or more years and then God allowed his house to be burned down and his wives and children to be captured before catapulting him into his promised position as king over Israel. Of course, the greatest example of all is Christ. Peter said, *"Christ also suffered for us, leaving us an example, that ye should follow his steps"* (1 Peter 2:21). Since they are our examples, there is no reason to think that the purifying trials that we must go through will be any less strenuous or easier to overcome than their trials were.

A excellent biblical example of this is the Thessalonians. They encountered persecution almost as soon as they heard the gospel and accepted Christ. Paul, the church's founder, was only with them three weeks before he had to flee from persecution. He was greatly concerned for their survival so he sent Timothy back to comfort and establish them in their faith. He explained his concern in the first epistle he wrote to them. He said he sent Timothy so *"that no one should be shaken by these afflictions; for you yourselves know that we are appointed to this. For, in fact, we told you before when we were with you that we would suffer tribulation, just as it happened, and you know"* (see 1 Thessalonians 3:1-5; Acts 17-1-10).

Why are we *appointed* to affliction? Because affliction has a specific purpose. It is a tool that God uses to humble, purify and perfect us. In fact, in spite of what some teach, the end-time church has to endure severe persecution before Christ returns. We must go through the Great Tribulation and defeat the antichrist before entering into the indescribable, unimaginable, Shekinah glory of the Millennial reign of Christ! (see Daniel 11:32-35; Revelation 6:9-11, 20:4-6; Romans 8:18).

Jesus comforted the disciples with this promise: *"These things I have spoken to you, that in Me you may have peace. In the world you will have tribulation; but be of good cheer, I have overcome the world"* (John 16:33). Once suffering has served its purpose, God brings it to an end. It doesn't last forever. We have this promise: *"Therefore humble yourselves under the mighty hand of God, that He may exalt you in due time... But may the God of all grace, who called us to His eternal glory by Christ Jesus, after you have suffered a while, perfect, establish, strengthen, and settle you"* (see 1 Peter 5:6,10). So, as Peter said, humble yourselves and patiently endure—your promotion may be just past the next offense—or not!

When Naaman came to Elisha to be healed of his leprosy, Elisha refused to even come out of his house and meet the visiting dignitary. Instead he sent his servant to tell him to go jump in the river! Once Naaman got over his angry temper-tantrum and humbled himself, he obeyed and was miraculously healed (see 2 Kings 5:1-14).

In conclusion, we see that it is by faith that God takes us through the open heaven process: by faith we ascend with Christ into the heavenly realms to abide at the Father's right hand (although we must first endure the fires of purification as we descend into our own personal, fiery designer hell—even as Christ descended into the literal hell—in preparation for the kingly anointing that we are to assume); *assume our kingly anointing and rule with Him over the powers of darkness.*

Then, with uncompromising holiness in our service to God, by faithfully praying the promises and decreeing the written decrees (an official order that has the force of law), *we judge with Christ and pronounce and execute His written judgments upon the wicked.* And finally, from this exalted position of spiritual authority, *we wage war with Christ until all His enemies are made His footstool,* and through the spoils of war reward the faithful with abundant provision (see Isaiah 53:12).

Jesus is waiting until, through us, He makes all His enemies His footstool before He returns for the church, at which time He

# The Church Triumphant

will purge the earth with fire, burn up the wicked and all their works before setting up His glorious one thousand year reign here upon the earth. In Paul's second epistle to the Thessalonians, he encouraged them with this promise,

> *We ourselves boast of you... for your patience and faith in all your persecutions and tribulations that you endure... that you may be counted worthy of the kingdom of God, for which you also suffer; since it is a righteous thing with God to repay with tribulation those who trouble you, and to give you who are troubled rest with us when the Lord Jesus is revealed from heaven with His mighty angels, in flaming fire taking vengeance on those who do not know God, and on those who do not obey the gospel of our Lord Jesus Christ. These shall be punished with everlasting destruction from the presence of the Lord and from the glory of His power, when He comes, in that Day, to be glorified in His saints and to be admired among all those who believe, because our testimony among you was believed* (2 Thessalonians 1:4-10)

# The Church Triumphant

# Chapter Eight
# Kingdom Culture

`Ralph Neighbor, the author of, *Where Do We Go From Here?* (a book about cell church), wrote, *"You cannot walk in another man's vision without first accepting his values."* This is true regardless of what that vision is. One might say that one cannot even *see* another man's vision without first sharing his values, much less *walk* in it.

Christ's vision of establishing a spiritual kingdom under His benevolent, Heavenly Father's authority, ruled with righteous judgment and justice for all (instead of establishing a natural, worldly kingdom that would defeat and dominate Israel's enemies, as the Jews expected Him to do), intimidated and greatly offended the religious leaders of Israel. At Jesus' trial they cried out to Pilate, *"We have no king but Caesar"*, but in truth, they were rebellious against both God and Caesar because they, themselves wanted to rule (see John 19:15).

Why? Because a king enjoys the honor of man, and they valued man's honor more than anything else. They desired the praise of men even more than God's. John observed that *"Even among the rulers many believed in [Jesus], but because of the Pharisees they did not confess Him, lest they should be put out of the synagogue; for they loved the praise of men more than the praise of God"* (John 12:42-43).

The priests and pharisees placed their affections on temporal, earthly things. Christ placed His affections on things above. Even Jesus' own disciples had a hard time overcoming the natural desire for the respect and honor of man. When Jesus told them that He would *"be delivered into the hands of men"*, they were so shocked by what He said and it was so foreign to their understanding of what the Messiah was going to do when He came that Luke tells us *"they did not understand this saying, and it was hidden from them so that they did not perceive it; and they were afraid to ask Him about this saying"* (see Luke 9:44-45).

Jesus understood that true, lasting greatness can only be achieved through faithful service and unselfish sacrifice, but His disciples thought it could be obtained simply by being in the right place at the right time. They thought that if they just stuck it out, when Jesus raised up His army and defeated the hated Romans they would automatically be promoted to positions of honor and be world–rulers. Then, anyone who despised them before they achieved their exalted titles and positions would be forced to honor them. Their vision was askew because their values were wrong.

The most enduring and difficult task that Jesus faced was convincing His disciples to accept His values. When He first revealed that He *"must go unto Jerusalem, and suffer many things of the elders and chief priests and scribes, and be killed, and be raised again the third day"*, Peter rebuked Him! *"But [Jesus] turned and said to Peter, "Get behind Me, Satan! You are an offense to Me, for you are not mindful of the things of God, but the things of men"* (see Matthew 16:21-23).

Before teachers can convince their students to accept the truths they hold dear, or leaders influence their followers to embrace the vision that they, themselves, walk in, they must first lay a foundation of values. When an individual or a society departs from their original values, their vision will change accordingly. So it is with America. She has lost her way because she has rejected Christ's eternal values and substituted her own, corrupt, temporal values in their place. And sadly, much of the modern, lukewarm, Laodicean church has accepted her values and is following in her footsteps.

## Kingdom Culture

What is culture? In a word, culture is a *value system*. Culture is what makes a society work. It consists of both written and unwritten rules of conduct that undergird and govern the actions of any given society. To abbreviate one dictionary's definition, *"It is the totality of socially transmitted behavior patterns and beliefs of human work and thought"*.

From the beginning, when God initially called Abraham out of his country, His intention was to use Abraham to raise up a great nation with a culture completely different from what he was accustomed to:

> *Now the LORD had said to Abram: 'Get out of your country, From your family And from your father's house, To a land that I will show you. I will make you a great nation; I will bless you And make your name great; And you shall be a blessing. I will bless those who bless you, And I will curse him who curses you; And in you all the families of the earth shall be blessed'* (Genesis 12:1-3)

Although the gospel transcends culture, in his epistle to the Corinthians, Paul spoke of a very important principle concerning ministering the gospel in other countries,

> *For though I am free from all men, I have made myself a servant to all, that I might win the more; and to the Jews I became as a Jew, that I might win Jews; to those who are under the law, as under the law, that I might win those who are under the law; to those*

*who are without law, as without law (not being without law toward God, but under law toward Christ), that I might win those who are without law... I have become all things to all men... Now this I do for the gospel's sake...* (1 Corinthians 9:19-23)

When we minister in other nations, to the extent that we can do so without compromising the gospel, it is important that we willingly and knowingly abandon our own culture and adapt to theirs. It offends them when we expect them to conform to ours.

When God told Abraham to leave his country, it was for this very reason. God commanded him to *"Get out of your country, From your family And from your father's house, To a land that I will show you. I will make you a great nation"* (Genesis 12:1-2).

Each kingdom develops its own culture, including God's kingdom. This world's various cultures are not always compatible with the gospel of the kingdom. Where there is compatibility, it is important not to interfere with the way others go about their daily lives. But in areas where there is conflict, it is imperative that we are careful not to adulterate or compromise the gospel.

Abraham's former cultural traditions and manner of living were incompatible with what God had in store for him. But it wasn't Canaanite culture that God had in mind for Abraham to learn to walk in—it was kingdom culture—and America's culture isn't any more compatible with kingdom culture than the idolatrous culture that Abraham was raised in!

Paul tells us that righteousness is imputed to those who *"walk in the steps of the faith which our father Abraham had..."* (see Romans 4:11-12). Before Abraham could qualify to receive the promise of being the father of many nations, he had to trust God and obey, leaving his former culture, family and inheritance behind. Likewise, before the American church can experience the full power and glory of the kingdom of God, it has to willingly forsake American culture and walk in kingdom culture, and these two are often quite antagonistic toward each other!

Jesus addressed one aspect of this issue when personal ambition caused sharp controversy and strife to arise among the disciples,

> *And He said to them, 'The kings of the Gentiles exercise lordship over them, and those who exercise authority over them are called 'benefactors.' But not so among you; on the contrary, he who is greatest among you, let him be as the younger, and he who governs as he who serves. For who is greater, he who sits at the table, or he who serves? Is it not he who sits at the table? Yet I am among you as the One who serves. But you... who have continued with Me in My trials... I bestow upon you a kingdom, just as My Father bestowed one upon Me'* (see Luke 22:24-29).

Pay close attention to what Jesus said to them about the kingdom as He concluded His admonishment. Obviously, He was telling them that the competitive nature of their former culture would not work in His kingdom. It wouldn't then, and it won't now! If we want to experience the fullness of the power of the kingdom, it is imperative that we recognize and embrace this basic principle.

This world's culture honors men by giving them titles and honorary doctorate degrees. The church isn't very different. Don't many of its ministers *"love the best places at feasts, the best seats in the [meeting place], greetings in the marketplaces, and to be called by men, 'Rabbi, Rabbi' [or Reverend, or Bishop]"*? (see Matthew 23:6-7). We are supposed to be honoring and exalting God, not ourselves! He said, *"Heaven is My throne, And earth is My footstool. Where is the house that you will build Me? And where is the place of My rest? For all those things My hand has made, Says the LORD. But on this one will I look: On him who is poor and of a contrite spirit, And who trembles at My word"* (Isaiah 66:1-2).

If we want to see kingdom power and glory, we must humbly learn to embrace kingdom culture. Jesus said, *"learn of me; for I am meek and lowly in heart"* (Matthew 11:29). Neither God nor His ways ever change. *"Jesus Christ is the same yesterday, today, and forever"* because in Him *"there is no variation or shadow of turning"* (Hebrews 13:8; James 1:17).

The world sells tickets to their events and many ministries and churches do the same. What about, *"Everyone who thirsts, Come to the waters; And you who have no money, Come, buy and eat. Yes, come, buy wine and milk Without money and without price"?* (Isaiah 55:1). Didn't Jesus talk about preaching the gospel to the poor? The poor can hardly afford to pay their electric bills, much less pay hundreds of dollars to attend religious crusades and conferences (see Luke 4:18). Jesus said, *"Freely you have received, freely give"* (Matthew 10:8).

In the kingdoms of this world *"Money answers all things"* (Ecclesiastes 10:19). With money, you can buy everything from a powerful muscle-car to a powerful, corrupt politician. If you have enough money, nothing appears to be out of reach, except, of course, God's mercy and power, as Simon Magus found out when he tried to bribe Peter. God cannot be bribed and His power cannot be bought (see. Acts 8:18-24).

Money has its place, but as Solomon wisely observed, knowledge and wisdom have a far greater, even everlasting value, *"For wisdom is a defense as money is a defense, But the excellence of knowledge is that wisdom gives life to those who have it"* (Ecclesiastes 7:12).

Although money is an important commodity in this world's economy, *faith* is the currency of God's kingdom, not money. In fact, James tells us that God has chosen the poor of this world rich in faith (see James 2:5). Could this be one of the reasons many of America's churches are so devoid of power? Because the services are designed to attract the wealthy (who have little faith) instead of the poor (who are rich in faith)? Be careful what you set your heart on. Paul admonished the Colossians with, *"If then you were raised with Christ, seek those things which are above, where Christ is, sitting at the right hand of God. Set your mind on things above, not on things on the earth"* (Colossians 3:1-2).

Many have discovered, much to their sorrow, that this world's culture seldom delivers what it promises. Even the *American dream* of being self-employed and independent—even when it is successfully achieved—seldom guarantees happiness. Many who have achieved it have also experienced what the children of Israel experienced when they lusted in the wilderness, God *"...gave them their request, But sent leanness into their soul"* (see Psalm 106:15).

Be careful what you wish for. Because we are in this world (though not of it), money certainly has its place, but it can also become a deceitful snare. Bot David and Solomon cautioned us about money, *"...If riches increase, Do not set your heart on them... For riches certainly make themselves wings; They fly away like an eagle toward heaven"* (see Psalm, 62:10; Proverbs 23:5).

After God finished creating the world He surveyed His creation and contemplated what He saw, *"Then God saw every-thing that He had made, and indeed it was very good..."* (Genesis 1:31). So, what went wrong, since everything around us definitely isn't *"very good"* now? Of course we know the answer. In the beginning God gave Adam authority over all His creation, which gave him access to glory, honor and unlimited wealth. Satan envied Adam's exalted position and schemed and connived to take it away from him,

> *For you [Lucifer] have said in your heart: 'I will ascend into heaven, I will exalt my throne above the stars of God... I will ascend above the heights of the clouds, I will be like the Most High'* (Isaiah 14:13-14)

Satan coveted Adam's glory and honor so he tempted and deceived Eve and outwitted Adam to get it through their submission to him. When Adam stepped out of his proper role as head of his household and submitted to Eve, through Eve, he became servant to the one she had surrendered to. Paul said, *"Do you not know that to whom you present yourselves slaves to obey, you are that one's slaves whom you obey, whether of sin leading to death, or of obedience leading to righteousness?"* (Romans 6:16).

Because Adam surrendered his God given authority to Satan, another spirit besides God's Spirit began working in and through His creation, and has continued to do so to this very day. Paul said,

> *And you He made alive, who were dead in trespasses and sins, in which you once walked according to the course of this world, according to the prince of the power of the air, **the spirit who now works in the sons of disobedience**, among whom also we all once conducted ourselves in the lusts of our flesh, fulfilling the desires of the flesh and of the mind, and were by nature children*

*of wrath... But God... raised us up... and made us sit together in the heavenly places in Christ Jesus* (Ephesians 2:1-6)

That which was created to be used for man's good and God's glory, Satan twisted and perverted to be used for his own benefit. Our task is to recognize his strategy and tactics and defeat him, recovering all that God gave Adam and restore it to its proper place and use. Honor, glory and money aren't evil within themselves. As for honor, Jesus said, *"If anyone serves Me, let him follow Me; and where I am, there My servant will be also. If anyone serves Me, him My Father will honor"* (John 12:26). And Paul also shows that honor is good as long as we seek it from God and not man. He said that God will render *"eternal life to those who by patient continuance in doing good seek [God] for glory, honor, and immortality"* (see Romans 2:6-11).

Likewise, concerning authority and its associated glory, Christ told the seventy, *"Behold, I give you the authority to trample on serpents and scorpions, and over all the power of the enemy, and nothing shall by any means hurt you"* (Luke 10:19).

And finally, concerning money, Moses told the Israelites, *"remember the Lord... for it is He who gives you power to get wealth, that He may establish His covenant which He swore to your fathers, as it is this day"* (Deuteronomy 8:18).

## Three Worldly Cultures

There are three worldly cultures, *Eastern, Western* and for illustration sake, I'll simply call the third, *Northern* culture. Previously, we defined culture as that which *"...makes a society work. It consists of both written and unwritten codes and rules of conduct that undergird and govern the actions of any given society."*

# The Church Triumphant

In a word, culture is a *value system* that has been established through tradition and is recognized and accepted as the norm by a given society. Eastern culture values honor above everything else, even above personal relationships. There, men will stone their children and kill their own wives if one of them brings dishonor upon the family name. On the other hand, Western culture values money over relationships. The pursuit of wealth and its associated pleasures comes before wives, children, friends and just about everything and everyone else, resulting in dysfunctional families and corruption in everything from government to industry.

Conversely, kingdom culture values relationships above both honor and wealth. The honor of man is vain and money quickly parishes but godly relationships are eternal. Kingdom culture is encapsulated in one word, love.

The tension between these three foundational, cultural roots — honor, wealth and relationships — is one of the primary causes of the constant conflict that is in the world. Why? Because each one has a different motivational force that drives it. The desire for honor is driven solely by pride. Lust for money and its associated material pleasures is motivated by greed and covetousness. Lasting, true, intimate relationships, on the other hand, are only obtained and maintained by love.

God's very nature is glory and honor and He already owns the world and all of its wealth. His heart's desire is to build a loving relationship with His children (see Hebrews 2:10). When the church compromises and attempts to build its kingdom on this world's values, it completely misses the mark and is assured of catastrophic failure. There is only one foundation that can endure the fire and that foundation is love. *God is love, light and life*, and when the church replaces love with the desire for man's honor and material wealth, it walks in darkness and death.

Jesus asked, *"To what shall I liken the kingdom of God? It is like leaven, which a woman took and hid in three measures of meal till it was all leavened"* (Luke 13:20-21). When love infiltrates the prideful Eastern culture based on honor, it humbles it, striking and defeating it at its very foundation because, *"Love suffers long and is kind; love does not envy; love does not parade itself, is not puffed up [and] Love does no harm to a neighbor"* (see 1 Corinthians 13:4; Romans 13:10).

Likewise, when the precious leaven (doctrine) of love is preached and practiced in the Western culture, it subdues and overcomes greed and covetousness, motivating its citizens to willingly sacrifice for the good of others (see Matthew 16:6-12; Luke 12:15).

Where the various combinations of the world's ideologies are dominant, such as in communistic nations, various monarchies and Islamic califates — and sometimes even democratic, capitalistic nations like America and Great Britain — personal freedoms are lost and many, if not most, of the families that exists in them are dysfunctional. Divorce, child abuse, addictions and poverty abound. Only God's kingdom has the potential of producing loving, close-nit families that truly prosper. Both Western capitalistic and Eastern monarchal and califate types of government are rampant with dysfunctional families.

But the third worldly culture which, for the sake of discussion, I've labeled *"Northern culture"* (I'll explain why shortly) is different from both Eastern and Western culture. Northern culture values *power and authority*. This value system is seen operating in communist nations like Cuba, China and the former Soviet Union. Nazism was based on this value system and the motivational force driving it is *the desire for Glory!* Lets examine two scriptural passages relevant to this subject,

> *Do not love the world or the things in the world. If anyone loves the world, the love of the Father is not in him. For all that is in the world — the lust of the flesh, the lust of the eyes, and the pride of life — is not of the Father but is of the world"* (1 John 2:15-16)

These three lusts were confronted and defeated by Christ in the Wilderness. I've highlighted certain points relevant to this discussion in each of the three temptations below. The first temptation was through *the lusts of the flesh,*

> *Then Jesus... was led by the Spirit into the wilderness, being tempted for forty days by the devil. And in those days He ate nothing, and afterward... He was hungry. And the devil said to Him, "**If You are the Son of God, command this stone to become bread**." But Jesus answered him, saying, "It is written, 'Man shall not live by bread alone, but by every word of God.'* (Luke 4:1-4)

Satan tried to intimidate Christ by *commanding* Him to satisfy His hunger by using His God given authority satisfy His lusts, instead of using it for God's glory, as it was meant to be used. When this tactic failed, the Devil alluded to *the lusts of the eye*, attempting to bargain with Christ by offering Him a "shortcut to glory"!

> *Then the devil, taking Him up on a high mountain, **showed Him** all the kingdoms of the world... And the devil said to Him, "**All this authority I will give You, and their glory**; for this has*

*been delivered to me... Therefore, if You will worship before me, all will be Yours." And Jesus... said to him, "Get behind Me, Satan! For it is written, 'You shall worship the LORD your God, and Him only you shall serve'* (Luke 4:5-8)

It is a mistake to think that Christ wasn't tempted by this lucrative offer. The Bible tells us that He was tempted in all points as we are, yet He overcame temptation and did not sin (see Hebrews 4:15). He refused to follow the easy route and instead chose to be faithful to His Father's vision. When Satan saw that both of his attempts to tempt Jesus failed, he changed tactics once again. This time he appealed to *the pride of life*, challenging Christ to prove that He was the Son of God by casting Himself down from the temple.

*Then he brought Him to Jerusalem, set Him on the pinnacle of the temple, and said to Him, '**If You are the Son of God, throw Yourself down from here**. For it is written: 'He shall give His angels charge over you, To keep you,' and, 'In their hands they shall bear you up, Lest you dash your foot against a stone'."* And *Jesus answered and said to him, 'it has been said, 'You shall not tempt the LORD your God.'* (Luke 4:9-12)

As one can see, the three temptations of Christ reveal the various lusts that motivate the three primary cultures that exist in the world today. *Western culture* is rooted in the *Lust of the Flesh,* where enterprising entrepreneurs endeavor to, and in many ways even succeed, in turning "stones into bread". Likewise, *Eastern culture* has its roots in the *Pride of Life.* In this system, honor is esteemed to have even greater value than life, itself. This is seen in the fanatical Japanese banzai charges and

# The Church Triumphant

Kamikaze attacks upon Allied forces in WWII and the Islamic suicide bombers of today.

But of the three worldly cultures, the most insidious of all is *Northern culture.* This culture is founded on the *Lusts of the Eye* and the motivational force driving it is the desire for *Glory*! Notice that Satan *"showed"* Jesus all the kingdoms of this world and promised to give Him *"all this authority... and glory"* if He would only worship him, which, of course, Christ refused to do. This was the temptation David succumbed to, and was later chastised for, when he ordered Joab to number Israel (see 1 Chronicles 21:1-8).

Likewise, Lucifer himself fell as a result of this sin and it is from his fall that I've named this culture *Northern culture* (in biblical symbolism, north means *above).* Isaiah said, *"How you are fallen from heaven, O Lucifer, son of the morning! How you are cut down to the ground, you who weakened the nations! For you have said in your heart: 'I will ascend into heaven,* **I will exalt my throne above the stars of God***; I will also sit on the mount of the congregation On the farthest sides* **of the north; I will ascend above the heights of the clouds***, I will be like the Most High' ."* (Isaiah 14:12-14)

The deceitful lust for money and its associated material pleasures is grounded in *the lusts of the flesh* (greed and covetousness). The insidious desire for the glory of having power and unlimited control over the people is rooted in *the lusts of the eye,* and the vain desire for honor is driven solely by *the pride of life.*

The tension between these three cultural value systems — the hunger for wealth and its associated material pleasures, driven by *greed and covetousness;* the thirst for power and dominion, driven by the desire for *glory,* and the desire for honor, motivated by *pride*—are the primary causes of the constant war and conflict that exists in the world today. Why? As we stated before, because of the different motivational forces and lusts that drive each one.

World History has proven that none of these three cultures are capable of producing true liberty and lasting happiness within themselves, but the desire for glory is especially insidious because it subjugates the people and brings them into total bondage and dependance upon those who lord it over them.

Why is it so important that we understand this? One reason is the political upheaval and turmoil that exists in America at this present time. At the time of this writing (2016-17), our nation is in the throes of a major cultural war—the forces of darkness are trying to shift us from a culture of freedom to worship as we choose and acquire wealth and property as we are able—to a culture driven by the lusts for power and glory by which all of its citizens will be enslaved and brought into total bondage to those who exercise dominion over them.

History reveals that, *without exception,* everywhere the Northern culture is dominant—in both socialist and communist nations—atheistic ideologies are enforced because Christianity is inherently antagonistic toward those who would usurp God's glory! John Witherspoon, a New Jersey cleric who supported the resistance just prior to the American revolution warned that *"there is not a single instance in history in which civil liberty was lost, and religious liberty preserved entire".*

Two things are common to all communist nations—atheism and disarmament of its citizens. Dictators fear the chastening power of prayer and the destructive power of guns. As they have been scornfully accused of doing, those who are wise and value their freedom will *"cling to their Bibles and their guns"*, indeed!

Islamic califates also restrict the freedom to worship as one chooses because, once again, true Christianity is incompatible with a society primarily based upon seeking the honor of man. Jesus said, *"I do not receive honor from man"* and, *"How can you believe, who receive honor from one another, and do not seek the honor that comes from the only God?"* (John 5:41,44). In both Eastern and Northern cultures personal freedoms are lost and many, if not most, of the families that exist in them are dysfunctional.

Crime, dishonesty and corruption in business and government, parents deserting their children, infidelity and adultery in marriages, unrest and rebellion among children in schools, violent gangs in the cities, terrorists executing Christians and performing mass killings in public places, all of these evils and more are the direct result of rejecting God's benevolent rule and values and replacing them with the world's ideologies. Truly, *"The wicked shall be turned into hell, and all the nations that forget God"* (Psalm 9:17).

Although the materialistic values of capitalistic nations like America, Canada, Australia and Great Britain also compete with the gospel (*"you cannot serve God and Mammon"* —Matthew 6:24), nevertheless, it is only in democratic societies like these that freedom of speech and personal freedom to worship is both esteemed and declared as an inherent right given to the people by their Creator.

Beware of those who, in the guise of being our *"benefactors"*, promote the Robin Hood mentality of taxing the rich and giving it to the poor. Their true (hidden) motive is to obtain glory by exalting themselves to rule over the people. Jesus addressed this evil when it arose among His disciples,

# The Church Triumphant

*Now there was also a dispute among them as to which of them should be considered the greatest. And He said to them, 'The kings of the Gentiles exercise lordship over them, and those who exercise authority over them are called 'benefactors'. But not so among you; on the contrary, he who is greatest among you, let him be as the younger, and he who governs as he who serves'* (Luke 22:24-26)

Satan worked strenuously in America through, *"the sons of disobedience"* in the 2016 presidential election—attempting to subvert our culture and turn it from a Western, capitalistic, free-market based culture into a Northern, power and glory motivated culture. He failed, but marginally so. With that in mind, we must diligently work to convert it into kingdom culture (love and service motivated). Power and glory belongs to God, alone.

In fact, everything belongs to God. He told Israel, *"Now therefore, if you will indeed obey My voice and keep My covenant, then you shall be a special treasure to Me above all people; for all the earth is Mine"* (Exodus 19:5). God called us out of this world's corrupt cultural system to be a special, chosen people to bring glory to Himself. He created us for that exact purpose!

*I will say to the north, 'Give them up!' And to the south, 'Do not keep them back! Bring My sons from afar, And My daughters from the ends of the earth—Everyone who is called by My name,* **Whom I have created for My glory;** *I have formed him, yes, I have made him'."* (Isaiah 43:6-7)

In both the previous administration and the 2016 election, Satan tried to usurp God's place in this nation and devote it to himself. Why was he nearly successful in accomplishing his dastardly deed? First and foremost, he infiltrated our education system with liberal teachers and professors who have deceived our youth into accepting his values. It is our job to reverse this trend by teaching and modeling kingdom culture in our homes, businesses, jobs and churches. Honesty, integrity, morality and justice have their own rewards and they offer a far more powerful and lasting benefit than the fleeting, temporal rewards of depravity, dishonesty and immorality: *"Godliness is profitable for all things, having promise of the life that now is and of that which is to come"* (1 Timothy 4:8).

Although changing a nation's culture is a complex task, we should start by saturating both our lower and higher educational systems with Christian educators to restore kingdom values to our youth. Even better — much better — home schooling and private, Christian schools should be utilized instead of the misguided, government run, public school system. Educating our children is our own, personal responsibility, not the governments. God said, *"**You** shall teach [God's word and commandments] diligently to your children, and shall talk of them when you sit in your house, when you walk by the way, when you lie down, and when you rise up"* (Deuteronomy 6:7).

Likewise, our corrupt political system must be purged and the various offices and positions filled with true, God fearing public servants instead of the corrupt, career politicians that hold office today. David said, *"The God of Israel... spoke to me: 'He who rules over men must be just, Ruling in the fear of God'."* (2 Samuel 23:3).

Christian entrepreneurs must be encouraged and financed to establish and operate morally upright, fair and honest businesses. Christians should boycott dishonest businesses and patronize those holding godly standards of conduct, even if they have to pay more for their supplies. Likewise, businesses that promote themselves through shameful, immoral advertising should be ostracized. Additionally, immoral, profane, R, X and even many PG rated movies must be abhorred and denounced! David said, *"I will walk within my house with a perfect heart. I will set nothing wicked before my eyes"* (Psalm 101:3).

Christians must stop endeavoring to be politically correct — receiving and loving man's honor but being utterly devoid of God's — we must become bold, radical, outspoken voices for God, abhorring and reproving evil while faithfully modeling righteous conduct. This is not to condone harsh, judgmental criticism of others, but we must walk in the delicate balance of truth *and* love — not just one or the other — as presently exists in much of today's Christian society. To please God and fulfill His purposes we *must* walk in love, but as Paul said, *"And this I pray, that your love may abound still more and more in knowledge and all discernment"* (Philippians 1:9). In fact, Paul gives us detailed instructions on this subject,

> *Therefore be imitators of God... And walk in love, as Christ also has loved us... But fornication and all uncleanness or covetousness, let it not even be named among you, as is fitting for saints; neither filthiness, nor foolish talking, nor coarse jesting, which are not fitting, but rather giving of thanks. For this you know, that no fornicator, unclean person, nor covetous man, who is an idolater, has any inheritance in the kingdom of Christ and God... Therefore do not be partakers with them... Walk as children of light... And have no fellowship with the unfruitful works of darkness, but rather expose [or reprove] them. For it is shameful even to speak of those things which are done by them in secret. But all things that are exposed are made manifest by the light, for*

*whatever makes manifest is light. See then that you walk circumspectly, not as fools but as wise* (see Ephesians 5:1-15)

## Honor, Glory and Wealth for the Kingdom

Three predominate cultures exist in the world today and all three compete with God for His tangible and intangible possessions—His *honor, glory* and *material wealth.*

*Honor,* whether it is used for good or evil, gives those who possess it influence among their peers. The *glory* of kings and business tycoons exalts them into positions and places of authority whether they use their authority either for benevolent purposes or for selfish gain. Likewise, *money* and its associated possessions equate to power; the ability to both get *things,* and to get things *done.* As one can see, all three, honor, glory and wealth can be used for good or evil, to enslave or liberate. I've previously discussed some of the harmful manifestations of these, so now let's briefly examine some of the positive aspects of each.

When acquired legitimately and used properly, honor enables people to influence others in a positive way, motivating them to serve their Creator and walk in love toward their fellow man. For example, *"And the Lord said to Joshua, 'This day I will begin to exalt you in the sight of all Israel, that they may know that as I was with Moses, so I will be with you'."* (Joshua 3:7). Of necessity, God exalts those whom He chooses to minister through. If a full vessel isn't lifted up, it cannot pour itself into one that is empty.

Likewise, authority and its associated glory gives one the right to promote order and administer judgment and justice in society. A prime example is King David, *"David reigned over all Israel, and administered judgment and justice to all his people"* (1 Chronicles 18:14).

# The Church Triumphant

And last but not least, those who possess money have access to the necessary resources to enable them to serve others in ways that simply cannot be done without it. Without a steady influx of money, foreign missions and outreach ministries come to a standstill and churches close their doors. Thankfully, God is faithful!

*And God is able to make all grace abound toward you, that you, always having all sufficiency in all things, may have an abundance for every good work* (2 Corinthians 9:8).

# The Church Triumphant

# Chapter Nine
# Mercy Verses Judgment

Just what, or who, does our Heavenly Father love, and does He actually hate some people? ("*As it is written, 'Jacob I have loved, but Esau I have hated'.*"—Romans 9:13). Does this verse actually mean what it says—or, as some teach, does it simply mean that God didn't love Esau quite as much as He loved Jacob? Doesn't the Bible teach us that God hates the sin but loves the sinner—and that He loves them all equally, with unconditional love? Or, is there more to this doctrine than we've been taught?

Although modern, *seeker friendly* theologians have muddied the water concerning this subject, the Scriptures are quite clear. Although God is indeed longsuffering toward sinners, His patience does have limits—and He does hate some people in spite of the heretical teaching that "*God loves everybody, including the vilest of sinners*", that is so popular today. Let's closely examine what the Bible actually says about this subject.

First, when the gospel is preached, God, "*sets His love*" upon those who choose to accept His offer of mercy and is long-suffering towards those who don't. But it is a serious mistake to equate His longsuffering (which allows sinners time to repent) with His acceptance of them or His approval of what they are doing! But what happens if, after someone hears the gospel, he or she continues to reject His offer of mercy? Will their rejection actually cause God to hate them? The answer is yes, it will! Love is a choice. God responds to us the same way that we respond to Him. David said, "*With the merciful You will show Yourself merciful; With a blameless man You will show Yourself blameless; With the pure You will show Yourself pure; And with the devious You will show Yourself shrewd"* (Psalm 18:25-26).

Even those whom God has set His love upon have to respond in like kind if they are to stay in His good graces. Centuries after the Israelites had settled in Canaan and the kingdom was divided, the northern kingdom (called Ephraim) turned from God to the worship of idols. For decades God warned them through the ministry of the prophets, commanding them to repent, but they stubbornly rebelled and clung to their idols. When God's anger finally boiled over, He said, *"All their wickedness is in Gilgal, For there I hated them. Because of the evil of their deeds I will drive them from My house; I will love them no more. All their princes are rebellious"* (Hosea 9:15).

When Abraham believed God and obeyed His command to leave his country and father's house and sojourn in a land that God promised to show him, his obedience justified God in choosing his descendants after him. After Moses brought Israel out of Egypt, he explained to them why God was treating them so special,

> *For you are a holy people to the LORD your God; the LORD your God has chosen you to be a people for Himself, a special treasure above all the peoples on the face of the earth. The LORD did not* **set His love on you** *nor choose you because you were more in number than any other people, for you were the least of all peoples; but because the LORD loves you, and because He would keep the oath which He swore to your fathers, the LORD has brought you out with a mighty hand, and redeemed you from the house of bondage, from the hand of Pharaoh king of Egypt* (Deuteronomy 7:6-8)

# The Church Triumphant

They were chosen to receive special treatment and attention, not by any merit of their own, but because their Grandfather Abraham had chosen to believe and obey God. Thus, they inherited not only the land that Abraham walked on but also the covenant, along with its many blessings and provisions, that God made with him.

In like manner, those who believe the gospel and obey its demands, through the adoption, inherit the covenant God made with Christ. Jesus met the conditions and fulfilled the requirements of the Old Covenant and earned every one of its precious benefits, then deliberately died to leave both the promised provision and the covenant to us as an inheritance. This cannot be over emphasized—every precious promise of the Old Covenant is contained in the New Covenant that we've inherited through Christ—for in Christ *all* the promises of God are yes and amen!

## The Gospel of Peace

God taught Moses the rules of engagement to use in warfare as he led the children of Israel toward their promised inheritance. He instructed Moses to always send an ambassador of peace to those He was sending him against. If they accepted his offer of peace, he was to make them Israel's servants, but if they refused, they were to destroy the males and take everything else as plunder for themselves. God instructed Moses to, *"When you go near a city to fight against it, then proclaim an offer of peace to it. And it shall be that if they accept your offer of peace, and open to you, then all the people who are found in it shall be placed under tribute to you, and serve you"* (see Deuteronomy 20:1-14)

In this Old Testament antitype, those who surrendered to Moses were spared. They became his servants. Those who refused his offer of peace and resisted were destroyed. This antitype is fulfilled in the preaching of the gospel. When Jesus sent the seventy out to preach, He told them to *"And heal the sick there, and say to them, 'The kingdom of God has come near to you.' But whatever city you enter, and they do not receive you, go out into its streets and say, 'The very dust of your city which clings to us we wipe off against you. Nevertheless know this, that the kingdom of God has come near you.' But I say to you that it will be more tolerable in that Day for Sodom than for that city"* (Luke 10:9-12).

Those who believe the gospel and accept God's offer of peace and willingly submit to Jesus as Lord are *"accepted in the beloved"* (see Ephesians 1:5-6). Those who refuse to accept His offer of mercy and submit to His Son are given time to repent. God is longsuffering. But if they continually harden their hearts toward Him and refuse to repent even after He repeatedly warns them about the consequences of their sins, He promises, *"He who is often rebuked, and hardens his neck, Will suddenly be destroyed, and that without remedy"* (Proverbs 29:1).

Suddenly destroying someone isn't an act of love! *"Love does no harm to a neighbor"* (Romans 13:10). Their destruction is clearly an act of God's wrathful judgment!

> *Therefore know that the LORD your God, He is God, the faithful God who keeps covenant and mercy for a thousand generations with those who love Him and keep His commandments; and He repays those who hate Him to their face, to destroy them. He will not be slack with him who hates Him; He will repay him to his face* (Deuteronomy 7:9-10)

God's attitude toward those who hate Him is seen in His response to King Jehoshaphat after he made a treaty with Ahab and went to war with him. Although God spared Jehoshaphat from being killed in the battle, He was angry with him for befriending Ahab,

> *Then Jehoshaphat... returned safely to his house... And Jehu the son of Hanani the seer went out to meet him, and said to King Jehoshaphat, 'Should you help the wicked and love those who hate the LORD? Therefore the wrath of the LORD is upon you'* (2 Chronicles 19:1-2).

If God loves those who hate Him, how could He reprove Jehoshaphat for loving *"those who hate the Lord"* without being a hypocrite Himself?

How do we know if someone hates God? The answer is simple! Those who love Him obey Him. Those who stubbornly refuse to believe and obey the gospel hate Him. John said, *"For this is the love of God, that we keep His commandments"* (1 John 5:3). Love is a choice. So who does God choose to love? Jesus, Himself, answers that question in a way that erases all doubt,

> *He who has My commandments and keeps them, it is he who loves Me. And he who loves Me will be loved by My Father, and I will love him and manifest Myself to him... 'If anyone loves Me, he will keep My word; and My Father will love him, and We will come to him and make Our home with him'* (John 14:21-23)

*"If anyone loves Me, he will keep My word; and My Father will love him"*. It cannot be stated plainer than that. The Father chooses to love those who obey His Son. To reject the cruel sacrifice His Son endured to unselfishly and mercifully atone for our sins grieves and displeases God beyond measure!

# The Church Triumphant

The unbalanced, overemphasis on God's love in today's churches has all but extinguished the sense of urgency to warn sinners of the wrathful judgment that awaits them. It has effectively quenched the evangelistic zeal that should be burning in every believer's heart. Sinners are sitting on death-row living on borrowed time, awaiting the date of their execution! Although God is *willing* to love them, they *will* be cast into hell if they don't repent and give their hearts to the Lord.

God created all things for His glory. We were created for His pleasure, not our own. Although He is merciful and longsuffering, He hates sin and sinners, alike. He is willing to love them if they will repent. But if they refuse to humbly submit to Him in repentance and glorify Him for mercy, invariably, they have serious trouble coming. Paul said, *"Knowing, therefore, the terror of the Lord, we persuade men"* (see 2 Corinthians 5:11; Romans 15:9).

Does the Bible actually say that God hates sinners? Yes, and in no uncertain terms! David, the man after God's own heart, who knew God's heart far better than most, said, *"The boastful shall not stand in Your sight; You hate all workers of iniquity. You shall destroy those who speak falsehood; The LORD abhors the bloodthirsty and deceitful man [and] The LORD tests the righteous, But the wicked and the one who loves violence His soul hates. Upon the wicked He will rain coals; Fire and brimstone and a burning wind Shall be the portion of their cup"* (Psalm 5:5-6, 11:5-6). It can't get any plainer than that!

If God wants to hate the wicked who choose to rebel against Him, that's His prerogative—but didn't Jesus tell *us* to love our enemies? *Yes, He did*, but He said to love them with *agape* love, not *philia* (affectionate, brotherly) love. Agape love isn't a feeling, it is a choice. In fact, if agape love wasn't a choice, God wouldn't tell us to love our enemies! So the issue isn't whether we are to love them or not—undeniably, that is required of us—it is *why* and *how* He said to love them that we should pay attention to.

To fully answer those two questions, *why* and *how* we should love our enemies, we need to examine what Jesus said in its context: *"You have heard that it was said, 'You shall love your neighbor and hate your enemy.' But I say to you, love [agape] your enemies, bless those who curse you, do good to those who hate you, and pray for those who spitefully use you and persecute you, that you may be sons of your Father in heaven; for He makes His sun rise on the evil and on the good, and sends rain on the just and on the unjust"* (Matthew 5:43-44).

So we see that first, Jesus is warning us to carefully guard our hearts against allowing hatred to fester toward those who do us harm. As Solomon wisely said, *"Keep your heart [pure] with all diligence, For out of it spring the issues of life"* (Proverbs 4:23). And second, instead of retaliating against them by rewarding evil for evil, we are to show them the Father's heart by doing good to them and praying for their conversion, giving them plenty of time to repent (which is exactly what the Father does).

Paul gave similar instructions to the Romans: *"Repay no one evil for evil... If it is possible, as much as depends on you, live peaceably with all men. Beloved, do not avenge yourselves, but rather give place to wrath; for it is written, 'Vengeance is Mine, I will repay,' says the Lord. Therefore 'If your enemy is hungry, feed him; If he is thirsty, give him a drink; For in so doing you will heap coals of fire on his head.' Do not be overcome by evil, but overcome evil with good"* (Romans 12:17-21).

It is evident that God is more concerned with the purity of our hearts than He is with either the salvation or the punishment of the wicked. (Having *"coals of fire"* heaped upon one's head isn't exactly a blessing!) Nevertheless, in due time He will punish them if they stubbornly reject His offer of peace and mercy and refuse to repent.

The Scriptures clearly show that our Heavenly Father's heart is to justify instead of condemn, excuse instead of accuse, bless instead of curse and save instead of destroy. Yet, He said that He *"will by no means clear the guilty"* (Exodus 34:7), so God has determined that those who harden their hearts and remain unrepentant after being confronted with the gospel are to be judged and brought to justice.

Those who preach the gospel of the kingdom are commanded to tell the people to repent. They must warn them of God's impending judgment, as Paul warned Felix. Felix foolishly procrastinated (see Acts 24:24-27). It is a foolish and dangerous thing to scorn God when He threatens judgment. Moses warned that if someone is obstinate and *"hears the words of this curse"* instead of repenting, he *"blesses himself in his heart, saying, 'I shall have peace, even though I follow the dictates of my heart'... The LORD would not spare him; for then the anger of the LORD... would burn against that man, and every curse that is written in this book would settle on him, and the LORD would blot out his name from under heaven"* (Deuteronomy 29:19-20 ).

To know God only as a God of grace and mercy is not truly knowing God. That is a very incomplete and unbalanced view of the King. His multifaceted character and transcendent attributes cannot be summed up in only one word, even if that word is love.

Truly God is both merciful and longsuffering but He will eventually punish unrepentant sinners with eternal banishment and torment, so God is both a God of love and compassion *and* a God of consuming fire! The Scriptures state that it is a righteous thing for God to visit tribulation upon those who trouble His people and scornfully reject His offer of mercy (see 2 Thessalonians 1:6-9). Moses summed it all up in one, long sentence! *"...I, the LORD your God, am a jealous God, visiting the iniquity of the fathers on the children to the third and fourth generations of those who hate Me, but showing mercy to thousands, to those who love Me and keep My commandments"* (Exodus 20:5-6).

# The Church Triumphant

# Chapter Ten
# Strategies for Change

*Ask of Me, and I will give You The nations for Your inheritance, And the ends of the earth for Your possession* (Psalm 2:8)

To disciple this nation, there are seven segments of society that are in need of ethical and moral reformation. Although successfully influencing and changing these seven may require different strategies for each specific area, there is one thing needed in every area, consistent, sincere, heartfelt prayer. Although there is no specified order, the seven segments are:

Government
Education
Family
Economy
Media
Arts & Entertainment
Religion

Because in the final analyst all ethical and moral behavior is a matter of personal choice, the various prayer strategies implemented to produce positive change should concentrate on individual character development in the *leaders* of each segment. *Wikipedia,* says the word *ethics* is derived from an ancient Greek word meaning *"relating to one's character"* and *Ethical* is defined as *"...Equitable, fair and just dealing with people that... conforms to self-imposed high standards of public conduct."*

# The Church Triumphant

A nation's government either directly controls or greatly influences every aspect of the peoples' lives. Solomon said, *"When the righteous are in authority, the people rejoice; But when a wicked man rules, the people groan"* (Proverbs 29:2). So, the key to efficient and effective spiritual warfare is: *"Fight with no one small or great, but only with the king..."* (2 Chronicles 18:30). When a nation's leaders fear God and rule in righteousness, the people under their authority are influenced and spiritually motivated to follow their example.

Although the goal is the same in each of the seven segments, the method for achieving that goal must be tailored to the specific, targeted area. For example, although at this present time both our government and Hollywood are influenced and manipulated by many corrupt and immoral people, bringing change to these two institutions will require two vastly different approaches.

Regardless of what area of society we concern ourselves with, in every institution where unethical rulers are unwilling to change and amend their ways, any successful strategy to bring about positive change requires replacing those obstinate people with those who *are* ethical in their behavior. In those cases, our prayer should be as King David's was, *"Let his days be few, And let another take his office"* (Psalm 109:8). God gave King David an important charge concerning governmental rulers. He said, *"The God of Israel said, The Rock of Israel spoke to me: 'He who rules over men must be just, Ruling in the fear of God'."* (2 Samuel 23:3).

It isn't enough to ask only for the removal of those who are corrupt, we must ask God to replace them with rulers who are just, fear God and hate covetousness. But before we go into detailed prayer strategies, let's examine the way the King of kings and Lord of lords makes His own decisions as He governs His kingdom.

## King Ahasuerus' Example

In the story of Esther, God shows us exactly how he operates His government. Theologians agree that Queen Vashti represents the Jews, Esther represents the church and Mordecai represents Christ as the Son of Man. But what is often over-looked is that, based upon the above pattern of interpretation, of necessity King Ahasuerus represents Christ as the King (the Husband of the Bride), and it is to him and his administration that we now turn our attention.

In this story, when Queen Vashti refused to honor and obey King Ahasuerus, he became angry and turned to His trusted counselors for their advice,

> *Then the king said to the wise men who understood the times (**for this was the king's manner toward all who knew law and justice...**) '**What shall we do** to Queen Vashti, **according to law**, because she did not obey the command of King Ahasuerus brought to her by the eunuchs?'*... [his counselors' advice was] *'If it pleases the king, let a royal decree go out from him... that Vashti shall come no more before King Ahasuerus; and let the king give her royal position to another who is better than she...' And the reply pleased the king and the princes, and the king did according to the word of Memucan* (see Esther 1:12,15,19-22)

This beautiful story clearly shows that God doesn't operate as a dictator. Rather than make a judgmental decision in anger, King Ahasuerus turned to his trusted advisors and asked for their counsel. Likewise, King Jesus listens to those He trusts and considers their concerns and counsel as He conducts the affairs of His mighty kingdom! Our prayers count! They are of the utmost importance.

## Imprecatory Prayers

Paul told the Corinthians that we should be ready to punish all disobedience when our obedience is fulfilled (see 2 Corinthians 10:6). Although no one is perfect, in the areas where we are walking in righteousness we can certainly ask God to put an end to wickedness in those areas! For example, we should pray daily for God to judge and bring conviction upon the Federal Supreme Court Justices who condone and abet abortion. We should ask Him to confront them and execute His written judgments upon those who harden their hearts and refuse to repent.

Although some Christians have resorted to public demonstrations and sit–ins to curb this outrageous slaughter (over 500,000 abortions each year), in spite of all their efforts, thus far they have been completely ineffective. Nothing is going to change in this situation until the church rises up and sends a strong and clear message of outrage to God! No longer should we ask God to show mercy upon corrupt, unrepentant governmental leaders. It's time for Him to extend mercy to their victims! This can only be done by God's divine judgment being executed upon the workers of iniquity!

Although the greater blame is upon the Supreme Court Justices, the doctors who murder babies aren't innocent, either. They've brought a curse upon the whole medical field. God said, *"Cursed is the one who takes a bribe [receives pay] to slay an innocent person"* (Deuteronomy 27:25).

The cry of innocent blood is going to bring God's wrath down upon this whole nation if the church doesn't rise up and cry out for Him to judge the individual perpetrators of this evil. Neither God, nor His judgments, ever change! He told Noah, *"Whoever sheds man's blood, By man his blood shall be shed; For in the image of God He made man"* (Genesis 9:6).

God's ears are ringing from the silent cry of the thousands of babies who are daily being sacrificed by the heartless doctors in America. God told Cain, *"The voice of your brother's blood cries out to Me from the ground"* (Genesis 4:10). If God's people don't send up a cry for selective, individual justice to be executed upon these wicked people the cry of our children's blood is going to bring total destruction upon us all! Isaiah lamented, *"No one calls for justice, Nor does any plead for truth...[therefore] Justice is turned back, And righteousness stands afar off; For truth is fallen [and is being trampled] in the street"* (Isaiah 59:4, 14).

America's children are being sacrificed upon the alter of convenience and the church is doing nothing to stem the ever-rising tide of destruction that is coming. America is like Israel of old; after they conquered Canaan and enjoyed the blessings of freedom and prosperity that God showered upon them for a season, they forgot God and adopted the ways of the people around them,

> *They even sacrificed their sons And their daughters to demons, And shed innocent blood, The blood of their sons and daughters, Whom they sacrificed to the idols of Canaan; And the land was polluted with blood* (Psalms 106:37-38)

If you study the etymology of the word *Canaan*, you will find that it originality meant "one who prostrates himself" and over time the meaning gradually changed to "one who bends the knee". By the time Israel invaded Canaan, it had evolved to mean "the pedlar". In other words, one who bows and worships financial gain (as in Baal worship), as many capitalists are prone to do in this day and time. This dangerous trend exists in many capitalistic, free-enterprise countries today. The fruit of capitalism is only good when those who practice capitalism walk in love and generosity. When greed and covetousness come into play children become a burden and are often sacrificed on the alter of "financial gain and success".

Abortion is deeply woven into the fabric of our society. Most abortions are the result of unwanted pregnancies that are the fruits of fornication and adultery. Fornication and adultery results from worshiping the creature instead of the creator. Fornication is to the mind what idolatry is to the spirit. In other words, fornication reveals and is a manifestation of idolatry and America is seeped in idolatry.

Can the church stop abortion? Paul said that we could if we would put our spiritual weapons to work *"For the weapons of our warfare are not carnal but mighty in God for pulling down strong-holds"* (2 Corinthians 10:3-4). Besides praying imprecatory prayers against the supporters of abortion, we should also ask God to reject all Judges who reject His word and exalt their law above His! He should remove those from office who refuse to permit our children to pray in school and call upon the Name of their Savior. He should oppose them and cast them out the same way they reject His word and cast out His commandments. Some good examples of imprecatory prayers to pray are found in Psalms 35; 52; 55; 58; 79; 109 and 137.

## Seven Segments of Society

Although I've separated society into seven segments for the purpose of developing effective strategies to promote positive ethical and moral change, in reality, the segments overlap and interact with each other. No one strategy will work alone. The following suggested strategies are given to provide purpose and guidance but are not meant to be exhaustive or exclusive.

# GOVERNMENT

*For the Lord is our Judge, The Lord is our Lawgiver, The Lord is our King; He will save us* (Isaiah 33:22).

In America, the most important segment of society in drastic need of change are the three branches of civil government; executive, legislative and judicial. Isaiah 33:22 (quoted above) reveals that in God's kingdom, not only in heaven but also on earth, Jesus fulfills all three functions — thus in this segment our prayers should be that His righteous government would be manifested and become firmly established on earth as it already is in heaven!

In many ways our government either influences or exercises direct control over all seven segments of society, including their own segment. Unethical, immoral people in government support unethical practices and promote and encourage immorality in the nation's citizens. As Isaiah said concerning Judah, *"For the leaders of this people cause them to err, And those who are led by them are destroyed"* (Isaiah 9:16).

For example, in direct violation of our Constitution, during the past six decades America's Supreme Court Justices have authorized the slaughter of millions of unborn babies, authorized the government to seize property from private citizens and award it to others if it will benefit the government with additional tax revenues, authorized homosexual marriages, forbidden the display of the Ten Commandments and Nativity Scenes in public places and has expressively forbidden prayer and other forms of religious expression in our schools, yet they have protected the right to publish and promote immoral pornographic films and magazines under the right of free speech! It has even reached the point that some verses of Scripture are labeled as *hate speech* and those who use them to preach against homosexuality are criminalized.

Previous Presidential administrations, with the aid of both houses of Congress, have burdened this nation with grievous debt beyond its ability to ever repay and continues to cripple its once mighty economy with ever increasing, ruinous taxes, rules and regulations.

Police corruption and abuse of authority is another area of government that is in dire need of reform. Although not all policemen are corrupt, some have become so arrogant and oppressive that severe animosity and hatred has been generated toward them throughout the nation. Although Paul said, *"Let every soul be subject to the governing authorities. For there is no authority except from God, and the authorities that exist are appointed by God"* (Romans 13:1). This includes the police, but when the police cease to minister for the good of the public and use their God given authority to prey upon the citizens, it is time for God's people to appeal to heaven and ask for justice to be served upon those who are supposed to be ministering justice!

God is righteous altogether! He doesn't approve of those who represent Him — those who are instruments of His justice — abusing their authority whether they do so in His Name or while denying His Name. Those authorities are subject to God's people if and when they pray as they should! Although we should ask God for their safety and protection, since they are

God's ministers, we should also pray for Him to discipline them when they become corrupt and abusive in their dealings with the public.

A simple example that everyone can relate to is this: when small towns lower the speed limit on four-lane highways passing through their city limits specifically to prey upon unaware motorists, that isn't a proper use of the sword God entrusted them with. It is necessary for the church to learn to pray *against* evil instead of only praying *for* good! It wasn't until Elijah prayed against Israel and stopped the heavens from giving them rain that they were willing to turn their hearts back to God (see 1 Kings 17:1, 18:39; James 17:18).

Even when God, in His anger, gives a governmental entity the authority to punish His people, He requires them to show mercy during the process. For instance, when He sent the Chaldeans to chasten Judah for her disobedience and grievous trespasses, He judged and punished the Chaldeans afterward because of their heavy-handed, unmerciful dealings with His people and lack of respect shown toward the elderly. In time, God brings every deed into judgment, and there is no partiality shown to anyone: *"Sit in silence, and go into darkness, O daughter of the Chaldeans... I was angry with My people... And given them into your hand. You showed them no mercy; On the elderly you laid your yoke very heavily"* (Isaiah 47:5-6).

Prayer is a *two-edged* sword! We should pray for those in authority, including the police, border patrol and even our military forces to be protected from harm. But we should also pray for them to be as merciful as possible while they carry out their God appointed duties, otherwise, they, too, should be chastened.

Respect is another virtue that is in serious decline in this nation. It has deteriorated beyond recognition in both the young and old, alike. Respect is a two-way street. When people in government cease to respect the people they are responsible to serve, they lose their respect in turn. This was clearly exemplified in the 2016 presidential election—Hillary Clinton arrogantly called Trump supporters "a basket of deplorables", and in turn was despised and rejected by those very same "deplorables"! Everyone reaps what they sow, and even intangible things such as respect and mercy are covered by that immutable law. Jesus said, *"For with what judgment you judge, you will be judged; and with the measure you use, it will be measured back to you"* (Matthew 7:2).

At present, America's governmental establishment, at every level, including federal, state and local, is so overreaching and corrupt that it is threatening the freedoms and well-being of every member of our society for many generations to come. Without doubt, this type of governmental abuse is one of the primary reasons Paul was inspired to write to Timothy with instructions on the proper way to start church services (although these instructions are largely ignored in many of today's churches),

> *I exhort first of all that supplications, prayers, intercessions, and giving of thanks be made for all men, for kings and all who are in authority, that we may lead a quiet and peaceable life in all godliness and reverence* (see 1 Timothy 2:1-2; 3:15).

Although every adult, American citizen, including all Christians, should take full advantage of our democracy and vote for morally upright candidates, voting is only part of the answer. You can't elect someone who isn't running for office!

# The Church Triumphant

The church has to pray for God to call and promote qualified leaders whom He has chosen. Then, once they are elected, we have to pray for them to faithfully do the job they were elected to do without conforming to the corrupt political establishment that existed before they were put into office. We cannot expect them to properly and successfully do their job if we aren't consistent in doing what God instructed us to do!

## Federal, State and Local

Both federal and state have all three branches of government (executive, legislative and judicial) but this isn't necessarily true at the local level. Local government tends to be more democratic in nature and the citizens have more direct influence in the day-to-day affairs of their officials. When possible, we should put legs to our prayers by calling or writing various officials requesting the desired changes we are praying for.

Influencing future election outcomes will involve persistent, daily prayer the same as it did in the 2016 election, but besides prayer, to reform government at every level we must openly and publicly support and promote morally superior candidates who run for office, including supporting them financially as much as possible.

In addition to actively promoting and supporting qualified candidates while they are running for office, we must continue to support them through prayer after they are elected. Also, our prayers must be based upon more than party preferences and personal political agendas, they must address issues that promote unity and peace within the nation. Remember, Paul said the purpose of praying for governmental leaders is so *"that we may lead a quiet and peaceable life in all godliness and reverence"*.

Our prayers should be aggressive and not defensive in

nature, as God told us they should be. He said, *"Ask Me of things to come concerning My sons; And concerning the work of My hands, you command Me"* (Isaiah 45:11). It should be obvious that God isn't telling us to command *Him* to do something in this verse—He is telling us to command and decree the judgments found in His word so that they will be manifested and executed in the earth. He is telling us to command these decrees *for* and *with* Him!

Immediately after executing God's judgement upon a fig tree for not producing fruit, Jesus told His disciples, *"Have faith in God. For assuredly, I say to you, whoever says to this mountain, 'Be removed and be cast into the sea,' and does not doubt in his heart, but believes that those things he says will be done, he will have whatever he says"* (see Mark 11:12-24). Although we may not see our prayers answered immediately, Jesus said if we believe, those things we ask for *will be done* and we *will have* whatever we say. God isn't telling us to ask and then ignoring our prayers when we obey and pray! Like King Ahasuerus, He is asking for and listening to our counsel.

For those who are timid or fearful in nature and hesitant about praying against corrupt leaders or are uncertain that they have the authority to pray against governmental officials that will not bow to Christ's commands, pay particular attention to the instructions contained in the following Psalm,

*Let the saints be joyful in glory; Let them sing aloud on their beds. Let the high praises of God be in their mouth, And a two-edged sword in their hand, To execute vengeance on the nations, And punishments on the peoples; To bind their kings with chains, And their nobles with fetters of iron; To execute on them the written judgment—This honor have all His saints. Praise the LORD!* (Psalm 149:5-9)

# The Church Triumphant

Although some think that this Psalm will only apply during the Millennium Reign of Christ, that view is completely erroneous. God's saints will be the *"nobles"* and *"kings"* during the Millennium, not earthly kings and carnal rulers! The Bible says that we will rule and reign with Christ throughout His thousand year reign (see Revelation 20:4). Obviously, this Psalm is for now!

The two-edged sword is prayer. The reason it is two-edged is that it is forged *for* righteousness and *against* iniquity. Also, take note that *"all His saints"* have this honor, not just those in high positions of spiritual authority,

Government affects everyone's life, both small and great. Since the authority to govern is granted by God, and everyone is affected by governmental policies, *everyone* has the right to appeal to God for Him to make those who govern operate according to His standards and not one of their own. (Is it any wonder why our government officials are doing everything they can to try to silence the saints and stop them from praying?)

How effective are our prayers in influencing government officials in the policies they make and the laws they pass? Far more than you might think! A good example of how effective we can be is John Knox. Knox was a Scottish clergyman who was a leader of the Protestant Reformation. He was imprisoned during the late 1540's for supporting the Reformation in Scotland. While in prison, Knox prayed daily, *"Lord, give me Scotland, or I die"*. By the time he died in 1572, Scotland had been transformed and the Scottish Parliament had adopted the Reformation doctrines. It is reported that the Queen of Scotland said, *"I fear the prayers of John Knox more than all the armies of England"*.

Knox was only one voice. What would happen if all of God's intercessors, with one voice, began crying out to God as He told us to do: *"Ask of Me [for America], and I will give You the nations for Your inheritance"* (Psalm 2:8). Why would He tell us to ask for our nation if He wasn't willing to give it to us? In fact, the *Passion Translation* interprets this passage as, *"Ask me to give you the nations and I will do it, and they shall become your legacy. Your domain will stretch to the ends of the earth. And you will rule over them with unlimited authority, crushing their rebellion as an iron rod smashes jars of clay!"* (Psalm 2:8-9, TPT). Is this translation correct? History shows that it is! Truly John Knox's legacy is a reformed Scotland, just as that translation promises!

One of our Government's responsibilities is to administer righteous judgment and justice for the people. Instead of justice, our government, at every level, has burdened America's businesses with ruinous rules and regulations and robbed the people through heavy taxation. There is little justice to be had, but it's not all their fault! Isaiah reproved Israel for not asking for justice. He said, *"No one calls for justice, Nor does any plead for truth"*. The church has fallen into the same grievous error.

It's time for God's people to rise up and appeal to heaven, asking Him to execute vengeance upon those who betray the public trust and live extravagantly and wantonly at their expense. The day has arrived for God's ministers to begin proclaiming both *"the acceptable year of the Lord, **And** the day of vengeance of our God"* (see Isaiah 61:2).

Peter said Jesus isn't coming back until everything the prophets have prophesied since the beginning of time has been restored and fulfilled. He said that heaven must receive Jesus *"until the times of restoration of all things, which God has spoken by the mouth of all His holy prophets since the world began"* (Acts 3:21). This includes the specific prophecies God gave about crushing Satan under the feet of His saints and making Christ's enemies

# The Church Triumphant

His footstool.

Jesus sits upon the Throne of David and *"David reigned over all Israel, and administered judgment and justice to all his people"* (1 Chronicles 18:14). Shouldn't we expect King Jesus to be even more competent at governing than King David was? We certainly should, and He will be if we will do what He told us to do. His honor is at stake: *"Righteousness and justice are the foundation of Your throne [and] The LORD is known by the judgment He executes"* (Psalm 89:14; 9:16).

In the parable of the unjust judge, Jesus exhorted us to ask God for judgment and justice to be served. This parable is peculiar in that in it Jesus placed a special emphasis on the condition of the church at His return. As the time for His second coming draws near, this parable, with its admonition to pray without ceasing, is even more relevant now than it was when it was given!

> *Then He spoke a parable to them, that men always ought to pray and not lose heart... There was in a certain city a judge who did not fear God nor regard man. Now there was a widow in that city; and she came to him, saying, 'Get justice for me from my adversary.' And he would not for a while; but afterward he said within himself, 'Though I do not fear God nor regard man, yet because this widow troubles me I will avenge her, lest by her continual coming she weary me.' Then the Lord said, 'Hear what the unjust judge said. And shall God not avenge His own elect who cry out day and night to Him, though He bears long with them? I tell you that He will avenge them speedily. Nevertheless, when the Son of Man comes, will He really find faith on the earth?'* (Luke 18:1-8)

# The Church Triumphant

God's people should pray for their leaders to conform to high, ethical and moral standards, or face God's chastisement. We must pray for those who faithfully serve the public as they should to be promoted to ever higher levels of honor and authority. But we should pray against those who abuse the public's trust and take advantage of their political power and influence to enrich themselves at the public's expense. Solomon said, *"The wise shall inherit glory, But shame shall be the legacy of fools"* (Proverbs 3:35). Those who abuse and betray the public's trust should be demoted and brought to shame and dishonor.

God works through the prayers of His children. He has adopted us into His royal family and formed us into a kingdom of kings and priests to serve alongside of Himself, (see Revelation 5:10). We have ministered in our priestly function in offering prayers and thanksgivings before the Throne, but we have failed miserably in executing the kingly functions that God desires for us to operate in. We must learn to exercise the authority and wield the sword that He has delegated to us. He has been patiently waiting for us obey and exercise our God given authority to judge those who rule over us!

If we are truly approaching the closing days of this age and nearing the time for the next one to commence as most discerning Christians think that we are—and there is an abundance of prophetic signs presently being fulfilled that indicate that we are—then it is time for us to become aggressive in prayer and radical in witness. God is seeking volunteers willing to fight alongside of Him as He wages war against His enemies. He is waiting for us to subdue them and make them His footstool. He asked, *"Who will rise up for me against the evildoers? Who will stand up for me against the workers of iniquity?* (see Psalm 110:1-3; 94:16).

# The Church Triumphant

Who, indeed? We should be more than willing to rise up and take a stand against Christ's enemies when we consider all that He has done for us! We should be eager to wield the Sword that He told us to use. For far too long we've been on the defensive. It is time to do what Paul said to do, *"And take the... [two edged] sword of the Spirit, which is the word of God; praying always with all prayer and supplication in the Spirit... for all [who are in authority, including spiritual authority, and for all] the saints"* (see Ephesians 6:17-18).

Below is a partial list of government offices and suggested subjects to use as a prayer guide:

**FEDERAL**:
    President and Vice President
        Cabinet
        Secretary of State
        Ambassadors
        Federal Law Enforcement Agencies
    Congress:
        House of Representatives
        Senate
    Judicial:
        Supreme Court Justices
        Federal Judges
    Military
        National Defense Preparation
        Troop Safety
        Peace from Conflict
**STATE**
    Governor and Lieutenant Governor
        House of Representatives

Senate
Judges
State Police

**LOCAL**

Major and/or Alderman
City Counsel
Sheriff and City Police
School Board
Police Juror

## Pray for God to:

Give our governmental leaders, at all levels, wisdom to conduct the affairs of government, without prejudice or partiality, for the good for all the people. Pray for them to interpret and uphold the Constitution as the original founders intended and not with a liberal, progressive agenda as many are so prone to do.

Expose and bring conviction upon all corrupt, wasteful governmental officials and remove and replace all those who will not repent and walk in integrity and morality.

Remove all federal judges, including those in the Supreme Court, who reject and oppose God and His laws and exalt their laws above His.

Judge and bring conviction upon all federal justices who authorize abortion and upon doctors who perform abortions and execute selective judgment upon all those who will not repent, that the whole nation parish not.

Provide protection for law enforcement officers and for the police to exercise their authority in a fair and equitable manner. For Police corruption and abuse of authority to be exposed and for corrupt officers to be judged, convicted, removed and replaced so the severe animosity that presently exists toward the police will be quenched.

Expose and remove all spies and moles in government, including cyber spies and espionage agents and provide the nation full protection from its many enemies.

Give all federal governmental officials a heart and the means to fully support and defend Israel.

# EDUCATION

Public education is extremely influential in shaping the ethics and morality of a nation. One strategy to change our failed system is to pray for God to reform it and restore it to its original purpose—to teach and train our children to live morally upright lives and to equip them to be competent, productive citizens when they reach adulthood.

Additionally, we should pray for God to give us school principals and board members who support Christian teachers (and at the collage level, professors), who teach proper ethics and morality but remove and replace those liberal teachers who oppose prayer and the teaching of biblical principles of morality in the schools. Our children must be taught about God and creation, instead of being indoctrinated with atheism and the theory of evolution.

As parents, perhaps we have failed in this area more than any other! Our children's proper ethical and moral education is our responsibility, not the responsibility of our government! Instead of home schooling our children we have surrendered them to a godless educational system run by immoral public officials and ruled by atheistic, Supreme Court Judges. God commanded us to *"lay up these words of mine in your heart and in your soul... YOU shall teach them to your children, speaking of them when you sit in your house, ...that your days and the days of your children may be multiplied in the land... like the days of the heavens above the earth"* (see Deuteronomy 11:18-21; *emphasis mine*).

## Pray for God to:

Have the Federal Courts put God and prayer back into America's schools and to obey the Constitution concerning not passing laws that control and restrict teaching Christian values and religious education in our public schools.

Promote godly people to lead both the Federal and State Boards of Education and give us righteous school board members at all levels.

Raise up and put into place godly school principals and teachers who will fight for and obtain the right to teach creation instead of evolution in school.

Expose and remove all corrupt and immoral school officials and teachers, at every level.

Give America's Christian parents the financial means, and both the desire and the ability to home school their children. Also for companies to publish godly home-school curriculums and make them affordable for Christian families to use.

Remove all liberal, atheistic college professors and replace them with highly qualified, godly, moral, Christian professors.

Raise up and prosper ministry training schools throughout the nation to train and equip evangelists and pastors for America's churches and missionaries for ministering in foreign fields of harvest.

Provide angelic protection over our schools to prevent both domestic and foreign terrorism from occurring on our school grounds.

# FAMILY

*Behold, I will send you Elijah the prophet Before the coming of the great and dreadful day of the LORD. And he will turn The hearts of the fathers to the children, And the hearts of the children to their fathers, Lest I come and strike the earth with a curse* (Malachi 4:5-6)

Although personal, moral conduct among families is a private matter, nevertheless, exerting a positive influence in this area is extremely important because the family is the basic building block of all society. Dysfunctional, unethical parents raise children who grow up to become dishonest employees, corrupt public officials, own and operate unethical businesses, etc. America's detention centers and prisons are filled with juvenile delinquents and men who were raised in fatherless homes. Fatherless families literally breed delinquent children who, in the process of searching for love and affirmation, join gangs and get involved in all manner of criminal activity.

Praying for fathers to take their rightful place of authority and shepherd their families as responsible parents should be a priority. This is especially true for pastors and youth leaders because their parishioners are greatly influenced by their conduct.

Besides prayer, proper ethics and morality among families can be promoted through proper education (as discussed previously). Churches providing marriage and family counseling services for troubled families is another way of helping in this area. Additionally, religious training and involvement provides a strong incentive for people to live morally upright lives. Contributions to churches and missions that provide such training is a good way to increase ethical conduct among the populous. Financing and supporting churches, religious schools and ministry training centers in impoverished areas will help increase morality in those areas. Cell church ministry is an excellent way to reach into and promote positive, personal growth in those areas.

## Building a Family Altar

The best way for parents to provide a covering over their children and keep them under God's benevolent, covenantal care is to establish a family altar in their homes. Satan has a hard time afflicting those you love when they are daily brought into God's presence through reading the Bible, taking communion and praying together.

For many Christians, the family altar consists of an entertainment center equipped with a wide-screen TV and DVD player. Although these things may keep us informed and abreast with the rest of the world, all too often they rob us of an intimate relationship with God. It's time for change, and today's pastors must lead the way! Paul even said that pastors are unqualified to pastor if they don't set the example by properly ministering to their families,

*A bishop [overseer] then must be blameless, the husband of one wife, temperate, sober-minded, of good behavior, hospitable, able to teach; not given to wine, not violent, not greedy for money, but gentle, not quarrelsome, not covetous; one who rules his own house well, having his children in submission with all reverence (for if a man does not know how to rule his own house, how will he take care of the church of God?)* — (1 Timothy 3:2-5)

# The Church Triumphant

The Greek word *proistemi*, translated *rule* in the above scripture doesn't mean to *dictate* but rather *"to stand before, to preside"* (Strong's 4291). Although most ministers teach that a husband is the priest of his home, in reality, he is not the priest but the pastor. In Christ, both the husband and wife are equal in their priesthood, but the husband is responsible for his family as a pastor is for his flock!

The Bible instructs the church's members to imitate their pastor's faith and conduct. Could this be one of the reasons there are so few family altars in existence today—the lack of proper role models? (*"Remember those who rule over you, who have spoken the word of God to you, whose faith follow, considering the outcome of their conduct"*—Hebrews 13:7). One church poll revealed that many pastors' daily prayer life consists of praying less than five minutes a day!

Besides following the faith and example of our pastors, both the church's pastors and members are admonished to *"walk in the steps of that faith of our father Abraham..."* (Romans 4:12). Observe God's testimony praising Abraham,

> And the Lord said, Shall I hide from Abraham that thing which I do; Seeing that Abraham shall surely become a great and mighty nation, and all the nations of the earth shall be blessed in him? **For I know him, that he will command his children and his household after him, and they shall keep the way of the Lord,** to do justice and judgment; that the Lord may bring upon Abraham that which he hath spoken of him (Gen. 18:17-19).

God's testimony commending Abraham reveals that if husbands want to walk in the fullness of the blessings promised by the gospel covenant, they must accept the responsibility to

# The Church Triumphant

*"command [their] children and household [to] keep the way of the Lord"*. Unfortunately, like Adam, husbands who don't properly govern their households will one day have to answer to God for their disobedience. When Adam chose to obey his wife instead of obeying God, he brought a curse upon the whole earth!

> *Then to Adam [God] said, Because you have heeded the voice of your wife, and have eaten from the tree of which I commanded you, saying, 'You shall not eat of it': Cursed is the ground for your sake...* (Genesis 3:17-19)

Obviously, Adam's sin of eating the forbidden fruit would not have happened if he had maintained his rightful place as Eve's head. He surrendered his authority over to Satan by submitting to Eve and brought a curse upon the whole earth. Through his disobedience, as we saw in the scripture above, the ground, itself, was cursed.

Although this curse is largely reversed by the Cross of Christ for all those who obey the gospel and faithfully walk with God, if we want to enjoy the blessings of Eden's abundant peace and provision, "obey" is the key word. Jesus said that just saying *"Lord, Lord"* isn't enough! (see Psalm 1:1-3; Matthew 7:21).

Accepting God ordained authority and responsibility doesn't automatically turn godly husbands who love their wives into tyrants and dictators as some fear. Far from it! Rather it empowers them to provide both security and provision for those they love and brings the family under God's loving, benevolent covering.

Although much of what I've written about the husband–wife relationship is an abomination to the modern feminist movement and is contrary to the American way of life, nevertheless the Bible clearly teaches that peace and stability are established in the home when men are kind and loving toward their wives and women are submissive to and respectful toward their own husbands.

When husbands take their rightful place and both husbands and wives have a heart to serve one another, they are walking in love and setting an example for their children that will forever be a blessing to them. So, set your hearts to obey and *"Through love serve one another. For all the law is fulfilled in one word, even in this: 'You shall love your neighbor as yourself.' But if you bite and devour one another, beware lest you be consumed by one another!"* (Galatians 5:13-15).

## Pray for God to:

Anoint Christian fathers to establish family altars in their homes and teach their children the word of God.

Save, train and equip *all* of our children to serve God, live morally upright, productive lives and be faithful witnesses for Christ.

Remove abuse and violence from America's homes and families and provide godly pastors, counselors, healers and deliverers who will minister to and heal both those who are abusive and those who are abused.

Provide godly, Christian spouses for our sons and daughters as they mature.

Prosper our adult children's families with godly prosperity (Pray 3 John 1:2 over your family: *"Beloved, I pray that you may prosper in all things and be in health, just as your soul prospers"*).

Bless our pregnant daughters and granddaughters with healthy bodies, healthy babies and easy delivery as 1 Timothy 2:15 and Deuteronomy 28:4 promises.

For spouses to love and serve one another and love and nurture their children, and fathers to honor their wives and wives to respect their husbands, as the Scriptures instruct them to (see Ephesians 5:33).

# ECONOMY

*And you shall remember the LORD your God, for it is He who gives you power to get wealth, that He may establish His covenant which He swore to your fathers...* (Deuteronomy 8:18)

All things being equal, businesses that treat their employees fairly and are honest in their dealings with the public prosper. Those who don't eventually suffer the dire consequences of their unethical dealings. James said, *"Come now, you rich, weep and howl for your miseries that are coming upon you! Your riches are corrupted, and your garments are moth-eaten. Your gold and silver are corroded, and their corrosion will be a witness against you and will eat your flesh like fire. You have heaped up treasure in the last days. Indeed the wages of the laborers who mowed your fields, which you kept back by fraud, cry out; and the cries of the reapers have reached the ears of the Lord of Sabaoth"* (James 5:1-4).

The above *"Lord of Sabaoth"* isn't Lord of *Sabbath*, but rather *Lord of armies*! (Strong's 4519). We don't need unions that are motivated by greed and operate in rebellion and witchcraft to correct this problem. Instead, the saints simply need to pray for God to send in the troops!

Supporting and promoting ethical businesses that already exist by buying their merchandise and stock and covering them with prayer is one way to ensure these businesses grow and expand their positive influence. Besides boycotting unethical businesses, we should pray for God to cut off funding to those who will not repent and treat their employees and customers as they should.

Besides ruinous taxes and regulations imposed upon businesses by federal and local governments, trade unions (as mentioned above), because of greed and corruption within their ranks, have greatly contributed to the failure of much of America's free-enterprise, economic system. Although unions were originally formed to promote the increase of wages and benefits and fair treatment of employees, instead of prayer, they have used the power of collective agreement to overthrow the authority of their bosses, turning things upside down. Employees who rule over their employers through the power of collective agreement are operating in rebellion and Samuel said that *"rebellion is as the sin of witchcraft!"* (see 1 Samuel 15:23). The spirit of greed and witchcraft is the driving force behind the corruption that exists within trade unions.

## Pray for God to:

Prosper America's economy and provide gainful employment for her citizens.

Remove all unnecessary taxes, burdensome rules and harmful regulations from America's businesses.

Expose, remove and replace all rude, corrupt and immoral business owners, managers and employees.

# MEDIA

*Now while Paul waited... at Athens, his spirit was provoked within him when he saw that the city was given over to idols... certain Epicurean and Stoic philosophers encountered him. And*

# The Church Triumphant

*some said, "What does this babbler want to say?"... For all the Athenians and the foreigners who were there spent their time in nothing else but either to tell or to hear some new thing* (Acts 17:1,18,21)

Like the philosophers Paul encountered in Athens, Americans worship the news. It has become an idol to many. Television, radio, newspapers and the internet compete for our attention and constantly bombard us with news, which often contains both true and false information, along with entertainment and advertisements. They exert a tremendous influence on our society and all are in dire need of ethical reform.

Entertainment and advertisements provided by television are extremely influential in the lives of children and adults alike. Many of the ads use partial nudity to sell the products they are promoting. The old adage, *sex sells* is true. It has helped sell sexual promiscuity to an entire generation of young adults!

American television news networks hit a new low during the 2016 presidential election, publishing fake news and unsubstantiated reports in an attempt to sway the election in favor of their liberal "democratic-progressive" (socialist) candidate. Even after the election, they continue to exhibit a strong bias against the President and his cabinet in their reporting. To paraphrase Paul, *"These lies must be stopped and these mouths closed, who subvert whole households, reporting things which they ought not, for the sake of dishonest gain and corrupt influence"* (see Titus 1:11).

Besides boycotting these networks and praying for God to withdraw funding from the news outlets that promote immorality, we should ask Him to prosper those networks who are fair and honest in their reporting. Praying for the production of quality, family oriented movies as explained in the following segment will also help bring about much needed change. Social media outlets such as *Facebook* should be used for promoting godly teachings and faith filled testimonies to influence others to serve God.

## Pray for God to:

Remove all political partiality from America's news networks, newspapers and news magazines.

Remove all news anchors who are dishonest and replace them with Christian men and women who are honest, unbiased and balanced in their reporting.

# ARTS AND ENTERTAINMENT

*Then they rose early on the next day, offered burnt offerings, and brought peace offerings; and the people sat down to eat and drink, and rose up to play [worship a golden calf]* (Exodus 32:6)

Although freedom of speech is a constitutional right in America, liberal Supreme Court Justices have sided with immoral producers of pornography and verbal filth to allow them to totally pollute the entire entertainment industry. Besides praying for God to convict and convert those justices, pray for Him to remove all who resist His Spirit and continue to support and defend immorality. We should also pray for writers and producers to produce more educational and entertaining books and films that carry messages of morality and integrity.

Producing inspirational films that promote godliness and morality have proven quite profitable to those who make them. The recent movie *War Room* is a prime example of this. *The*

*Passion of Christ* produced by Mel Gibson was one of the most life changing films of all time and was extremely profitable. Both of these films strike at the heart of the issue of unethical and immoral behavior.

Popular sports such as football and basketball have become big business in the US and, as is often the case, along with the enormous wealth they generate they spawn an abundance of immorality and corruption. Recent, scandalous, Super Bowl half-time shows are prime examples. Instead of watching and being entertained by this public display of licentious behavior, the saints should be praying for God to put an end to it!

## Pray for God to:

Bankrupt every business in the entertainment industry that produces, publishes and distributes pornographic materials, shows and movies.

Raise up and inspire Christian writers, movie producers and directors to produce inspirational and entertaining religious shows and godly movies.

Send a powerful revival to save and convert actors, producers and directors to transform the movie and television industry from "the love of money" to the love of God and godly relationships.

# RELIGION

Although I've placed religion at the end of this discussion, it is actually the *only* proven, infallible measuring stick available to establish proper ethical and moral behavior in the earth. History has proven that godlessness and immorality go hand in hand. Without a proven, universal standard by which to judge right and wrong conduct, there is no unit of measurement available to properly judge ethics and morality (everyone simply does what is right in their own eyes, which is condemned by the law; see Deuteronomy 12:8). The Bible, alone, provides a universal standard by which all conduct may be judged (and will be judged when each person stands before his or her creator on judgement day). There is no higher standard for promoting godly conduct than the biblical admonitions to *"Love your neighbor as yourself"* and *"Do unto others as you would have them do unto you"*.

As previously discussed under FAMILY, one specific segment of America's society greatly in need of ethical and moral reform is found in America's prisons. One suggestion to bring about positive change in this area is to both pray for and support prison ministries that have proven results.

Most prison ministry is done by small, unfunded ministries who are in much need of Bibles and religious books to distribute among the inmates. They need both prayer and financial support to be effective in their ministry. Prison libraries can be given religious materials to exert a positive influence on the lives of the inmates who use them.

Christian ministers who are involved in prison ministry are especially effective in changing prisoners' world view and lifestyles, enabling them to become productive citizens instead of returning to a life of crime once they are released. A true, born-again religious experience changes hardened criminals, homosexuals, thieves, etc., into moral, productive citizens. Many prison converts become ministers themselves, going back into the prison system to minister to their former cell-mates.

I can testify from personal experience that many dedicated missionaries also need a lot more prayer and financial support than they presently have. Christian missionaries exert a tremendous, positive influence for righteousness regardless of what country they work in. Most work at their own expense without support from those they minister to. Besides faithfully praying for them, we should also help them financially as much as possible.

## Pray for God to:

Established His righteous kingdom in the earth in full power and glory and for His good and perfect will to be done throughout the earth even as it is in heaven, in all seven areas of society.

Restore everything that has been lost and stolen from the church from ages past, including resurrection power and glory, and restore the ancient paths to walk in and landmarks to live by (see Jeremiah 6:16; Proverbs 22:28).

Raise up the righteous foundations for many generations to come. (Fasting is an important part of this intercession—see Isaiah 58:6-12).

Raise up and financially support and prosper faithful ministers and ministries who teach, preach and publish the unadulterated truth.

Provide angelic protection and assistance for ministers and missionaries who must travel both at home and abroad to preach the gospel.

Give pastors and ministers the boldness to preach the gospel of the kingdom as it should be preached, without compromise— regardless of opposition, and for them to preach the full, balanced truth, including the necessity for Christians to live in true holiness as godly examples to the world.

For the Lord of the harvest to send many qualified labors into the harvest fields to save, heal and deliver multitudes of lost souls who would otherwise spend eternity in everlasting torment (see Luke 10:2; Revelation 20:12-15).

## Conclusion

In conclusion, it may be noted that many of the various strategies suggested in this plan of action for ethical and moral societal transformation have been tried and proven effective many times over. The difference is that before this, no one has ever presented a comprehensive strategy with the sole purpose of exerting a positive influence upon the moral climate of the nation. If these various and sundry prayer strategies are faithfully implemented and consistently applied, they will accomplish much toward bringing America back to the ethical and moral standards that once made her great.

# The Church Triumphant

# Chapter Eleven
## Rules of Engagement

*And from the days of John the Baptist until now the kingdom of heaven suffers violence, and the violent take it by force* (Matthew 11:12)

Paul told the Athenians that God *"has made from one blood every nation of men to dwell on all the face of the earth, and has determined their preappointed times and the boundaries of their dwellings"* (Acts 17:26). God knows the end of all things from the beginning, and as Paul said, He has predetermined to make certain things transpire at *preappointed times.* As God progressively unfolds and reveals His agenda, so that we won't be caught by surprise, God gives us signs so that we will know when each specific time has arrived.

For example, Paul said, *"when the fullness of the time had come, God sent forth His Son, born of a woman, born under the law"* (Galatians 4:4). Although God gave the Jews several signs to announce the Messiah's coming and many miracles to confirm His presence, they still failed to recognize Him because He didn't conform to their doctrine—*but their doctrine was wrong!* Israel wasn't expecting their Messiah to do what Jesus did. They were taught that He would come as a powerful, conquering King who would establish a natural, everlasting kingdom in Israel (and at God's preappointed time, He will), instead He came as a humble, suffering servant. Since they misinterpreted the Scriptures and weren't open to correction, they completely missed *"the time of their visitation"* (see Luke 19:44; ). Today's church is in the same predicament. They've been taught and are expecting the rapture to occur at any moment but God's got something completely different on His mind. He is coming *to* the church to establish His kingdom *through* the church before He returns *for* the church!

During King David's reign some of his advisers were *"sons of Issachar [who] had understanding of the times, to know what Israel ought to do"* (1 Chronicles 12:32). God has some "sons of Issachar" today, too. In fact, there are many prophets in this hour who are all hearing the same thing and with one voice proclaiming — *"It is time for war"*. It's time for the God's people to wake up and pray for Him to rise up and do what He promised to do long ago — to utterly crush Satan under their feet!

War, by its very nature, is violent and destructive. Nevertheless, to prevent soldiers from inadvertently committing war crimes and similar atrocities, certain rules of engagement are often established before they are sent into battle. Natural things often mirror or foreshadow spiritual things. Thus it is in this case. The wisdom of God has established rules for engaging in spiritual warfare to ensure that His soldiers fight lawfully and stay out of trouble. Although our weapons are mighty, our warfare is against invisible principalities and powers who war in heavenly places, so to be effective we must be extra careful to follow the biblical rules of engagement that God has laid out in His word (see 2 Corinthians 10:3-4; Ephesians 6:12).

Since judgment begins in the house of God, the first rule we need to observe concerns judging those who are our fellow members of the Body of Christ. Paul said, *"Brethren, if a man is overtaken in any trespass, you who are spiritual restore such a one in a spirit of gentleness, considering yourself lest you also be tempted"* (Galatians 6:1). Stern, self-righteous judgment will invariably come back upon the one who judges because Jesus said, *"For with what judgment you judge, you will be judged; and with the measure you use, it will be measured back to you"* (Matthew 7:2). Hosea wisely said, *"Sow for yourselves righteousness; Reap in mercy"*. And Jesus echoed this advise with *"Do not judge according to appearance, but judge with righteous judgment"* (see Hosea 10:12; John 7:24).

When judging others, it is always better to err on the side of mercy than it is to render an unrighteous, unjust verdict. Nevertheless, since there are no benign sins and all sin has adverse consequences, sin cannot be simply ignored or justified. If, when church members are confronted (either directly or by God's divine intervention into their affairs through our prayers), they persist in their sins and will not repent, their sins must be exposed and dealt with properly or the whole church will suffer the consequences.

When one member is blessed, everyone rejoices with him. Likewise, when one member sins and does not repent, their sin adversely affects the whole church. This principle is revealed in the beginning of Joshua's campaign against Canaan when he fought against Jericho. During that battle a soldier named Achan secretly stole some of the spoils that were dedicated to God. His sin caused the whole army to lose the next battle they were engaged in. After his sin was properly judged and justice was served, Joshua's army was victorious over their enemies (see Joshua 2:7-8:26).

The second rule concerns something Moses covered in the law — when a trespass has been committed, sometimes there are varying degrees of guilt. In other words, although someone may be truly guilty of a specific trespass, he or she may not be the only one who should be punished. After Moses ordained elders to judge disputes between brethren in Israel, he told them, *"If a matter arises which is too hard for you to judge, between degrees of guilt for bloodshed, between one judgment or another, or between one punishment or another, matters of controversy within your gates, then you shall arise and go... to the judge [priests then, apostles now] there in those days, and inquire of them; they shall pronounce upon you the sentence of judgment... And you shall be careful to do according to all that they order you"* (see Deuteronomy 17:8:11; Acts 15:6-19).

If you are the one being accused (and you are guilty as charged), as Moses said, *"be careful to do according to all that they order you"* so that God can clear your record and set you free from the adverse consequences of your trespass. Being a Christian will not automatically give you immunity when your trespass is brought before God's Judgment seat. Paul said, *"But he who does wrong will be repaid for what he has done, and there is no partiality"* (Colossians 3:25).

Jesus said that when your brother has an offence against you, go and *"be reconciled to your brother... [either by declaring and explaining your innocence or by making amends and asking him to forgive you]. Agree with your adversary quickly, while you are on the way with him [when you are in the wrong], lest your adversary deliver you to the judge, the judge hand you over to the officer, and you be thrown into prison. Assuredly, I say to you, you will by no means get out of there till you have paid the last penny"* (see Matthew 5:23-26).

The third rule places limitations upon those who must pronounce the sentence of judgment upon those who are guilty of wrongdoing. This rule applies to sentencing believers and nonbelievers, alike. Without doubt, it is the most important rule of all! Isaiah spelled this one out for us in no uncertain terms! He warns, *"Woe to those who decree unrighteous decrees, Who write misfortune, Which they have prescribed"* (Isaiah 10:1).

# The Church Triumphant

It is not left up to our discretion as to what someone's proper punishment should be. God has already prescribed the correct penalty for each type of sin, so we should only pronounce *His* judgments, never those of our own making! In reality, because it is often impossible to know what someone's reasons and motives are when they commit wrong—and to what "degree of guilt" they share in the trespass (as we discussed above)—we seldom know for certain what their just punishment should be, and in many cases, we don't have to know. Usually, we need only pray for their iniquity to be exposed and justice to be served. God said, *"Vengeance is Mine, and recompense; Their foot shall slip in due time; For the day of their calamity is at hand, And the things to come hasten upon them"* (Deuteronomy 32:35). It isn't necessary or wise to tell God how to do His job! He is fully aware of what needs to be done so that justice will be timely and properly served.

What "woe" is Isaiah declaring in the scripture above, when he said, *"Woe to those who decree unrighteous decrees"*? The answer to this question is found in Moses' law: *"If a false witness rises against any man to testify against him of wrongdoing... the judges shall make careful inquiry, and indeed, if the witness is a false witness, who has testified falsely against his brother, **then you shall do to him as he thought to have done to his brother"*** (see Deuteronomy 19:16-19). This woe also applies when the witness is true but the requested or intended penalty is excessive or unjust. So, when in doubt, leave the penalty out!

In light of all this, wouldn't it be wiser to just live our lives in righteousness and leave all this judging stuff up to God? The answer is a resounding *NO!* As we discussed before, it is never wrong or out of order *or unsafe* to cry out for justice! Isaiah lamented because sin wasn't being opposed and restrained in

# The Church Triumphant

Israel. He said, *"No one calls for justice, Nor does any plead for truth... [therefore] Justice is turned back, And righteousness stands afar off; For truth is fallen [and is trampled] in the street, And equity cannot enter. So truth fails, And he who departs from evil makes himself a prey. Then the LORD saw it, and it displeased Him That there was no justice"* (Isaiah 59:4,14-15). God was grieved because there was no justice being served! Obviously, He wants justice to be executed even more than we do! God hates it when people trespass and needlessly offend one another—especially when someone takes advantage of and oppresses those who are weak and defenseless. In fact, He said, *"For I, the LORD, **love** justice"* (Isaiah 61:8).

It is absolutely necessary for the saints to pray for justice or truth will continue to be trampled under foot by the wicked. For example, when Paul's ministry was opposed by Alexander the coppersmith, he warned Timothy, *"Alexander the coppersmith did me much harm. May the Lord repay him according to his works. You also must beware of him, for he has greatly resisted our words"* (2 Timothy 4:14-15). Paul's, *"May the Lord repay him according to his works"* is an imprecatory prayer! God is waiting for our prayers so that He will be justified in administering a just and sudden recompense upon their heads! (see Jeremiah 23:19-20). The wicked continually travail for wickedness. Therefore, the righteous should unceasingly travail and cry out for justice!

So, when it *is* important to ask for a specific judgment to be carried out upon someone—as in church disciplinary measures, disputes between brethren, etc.—what are we supposed to ask for, and what are the acceptable decrees to decree? Besides the many prayers, judgments and decrees contained in the Psalms, one way to understand God's righteous judgments is to study Moses' law. Paul said, *"But we know that the law is good if one uses*

160

*it lawfully, knowing this: that the law is not made for a righteous person, but for the lawless and insubordinate, for the ungodly and for sinners, for the unholy and profane ...for fornicators, for sodomites, for kidnappers, for liars, for perjurers, and if there is any other thing that is contrary to sound doctrine"* (see 1 Timothy 1:8-11). Also, when applicable, the fines and imprisonments imposed by civil law are also appropriate penalties to pray.

Although all sincere, born-again, baptized believers are free from the law's carnal ordinances and commandments, along with its penalties, all unbelieving, unrepentant sinners will be judged—either by the letter of the law if they are Jews, or by the spirit of the law if they are Gentiles—when they appear before God, and they are all subject to its judgments and punishments while they are still living in this life (see Romans 6:3,14; 2:12,16; Colossians 2:14).

So, when corrupt public officials or federal judges do things like authorize unborn children to be slaughtered or pass laws that forbid our children to pray in school, their evil deeds should to be brought before the Judgment seat of the King to be dealt with. Their wickedness must be stopped to make room for righteousness to reign. God is waiting for you in the War Room. Are you coming?

*"The Lord is known by the judgment He executes; The wicked is snared in the work of his own hands"* (Psalm 9:16).

# The Church Triumphant

# Chapter Twelve
# The Restoration of All Things

Shortly after Peter raised up the lame man at the Gate Beautiful, he commanded those who witnessed the man's instant restoration to perfect health to *"Repent therefore and be converted, that your sins may be blotted out, so that times of refreshing may come from the presence of the Lord, and that He may send Jesus Christ, who was preached to you before, whom heaven must receive until the times of restoration of all things, which God has spoken by the mouth of all His holy prophets since the world began"* (see Acts 3:1-21).

It isn't coincidental that Peter spoke of *"the times of restoration of all things"* in the immediate aftermath of the lame man's restoration to perfect health. Among many other things, God's mighty, miraculous healing power is something the church lost centuries ago that must be fully restored. Malachi also prophesied of this glorious day of restoration: *"But to you who fear My name The Sun of Righteousness shall arise With healing in His wings; And you shall go out And grow fat like stall-fed calves. You shall trample the wicked, For they shall be ashes under the soles of your feet On the day that I do this, Says the LORD of hosts"* (Malachi 4:2-3).

Ever since God birthed the church Satan has done exactly what Jesus said he came to do—*steal, kill and destroy* (see John 10:10). He has worked diligently to *steal* the truth from the church to bring her into bondage *(the truth makes you free)*. He has *killed* her members through persecution, war and disease. And throughout the ages he has effectively *destroyed* her power and influence by infiltrating her congregations with false brethren and her pulpits with hirelings and wolves in sheep's clothing. He has introduced many false doctrines (doctrines of demons) and adulterated many others. Since her birth he has continually stirred up strife and division between brethren to hinder her growth and progress. Paul condensed it this way, *"And this occurred because of false brethren secretly brought in (who came in by stealth to spy out our liberty which we have in Christ Jesus, that they might bring us into bondage)"* —(Galatians 2:4).

The time has come for God to do what He promised. The church has a promise that goes all the way back to Genesis. In the beginning God told Satan, *"I will put enmity between you and the woman [Jew], and between your seed and her Seed [Christ]; He shall bruise your head, and you shall bruise His heel"* and Paul echoed this with *"And the God of peace will crush Satan under your feet shortly"* (Genesis 3:15; Romans 16:20). The church has waited and longed for God to fulfill these two prophetic promises for centuries, and that day has arrived. Paul's 2000 year old *shortly* is finally here!

The Jews waited for their Messiah to come for over a thousand years before He appeared. They waited so long that when He finally came they couldn't believe that He was actually there. Jesus scolded them with, *"When it is evening you say, 'It will be fair weather, for the sky is red'; and in the morning, 'It will be foul weather today, for the sky is red and threatening.' Hypocrites! You know how to discern the face of the sky, but you cannot discern the signs of the times"* (Matthew 16:2-3). Many of God's people are struggling with that same spirit of unbelief in this day and time. Be careful that you are not one of them!

God is reintroducing and restoring the gospel of the kingdom to the church. It is one of those doctrines that Satan stole as soon as he could get his hands on it! Why? Because it spells his demise. It both proclaims and accomplishes his complete humiliation and utter defeat. It is God's extraordinary, miraculous power operating in and through His humble, ordinary children. Paul said, *"For we have this treasure in earthen vessels, that the excellence of the power may be of God and not of us"* (2 Corinthians 4:7).

Herod beheaded John the Baptist and *"From that time Jesus began to preach and to say, 'Repent, for the kingdom of heaven is at hand'."* (Matthew 4:17). Why did Jesus wait until John was beheaded before He started preaching the kingdom? Because John represented the law. Jesus said, *"And from the days of John the Baptist until now the kingdom of heaven suffers violence, and the violent take it by force. For all the prophets and the law prophesied until John"* (Matthew 11:12-13).

John represented Moses' law and his head represented the law's authority. God removed the law and replaced it with Christ and His law! Moses' law was carnal. Christ's law is spiritual. *"The law of sin and death"* was weak but the *"law of the spirit of life in Christ Jesus"*, is *"mighty through God to the pulling down of strongholds"*. (see Romans 8:2-3; 2 Corinthians 10:4). The time has come for God to restore all things spoken by the prophets from the beginning of creation. It is time for the church, *with* Christ, to manifest the *full* gospel to the world, the mighty gospel of the eternal kingdom of God.

> *Behold, the Lord GOD shall come with a strong hand, And His arm shall rule for Him; Behold, His reward is with Him, And His work before Him* (Isaiah 40:10)

# The Church Triumphant

# Appendix
# The Doctrine of Baptisms

*Therefore, leaving the discussion of the elementary principles of Christ, let us go on to perfection, not laying again the foundation of repentance from dead works and of faith toward God, of the doctrine of baptisms, of laying on of hands, of resurrection of the dead, and of eternal judgment* (Hebrews 6:1-2)

A careful study of the Bible reveals that God has purposed to baptize His people with seven specific baptisms before He returns. In order, they are the Baptism of,

Repentance from Dead Works
Faith toward God
Water (Separation)
Holy Spirit
Fire I (Resurrection Power)
Fire II (Purification)
Suffering and (Willing) Sacrifice

## The Baptism of Repentance

John the Baptist introduced the baptism of repentance in preparation for the first coming of Christ and His appearing to Israel. *"And [John] came into all the country about Jordan, preaching the baptism of repentance for the remission of sins"* (Luke 3:3). John's message included something that is seldom heard from modern pulpits today, the necessity of repenting and confessing one's sins once we accept Christ's offer of mercy and forgiveness! *"And [they] were baptized of [John] in Jordan, confessing their sins"* (Matthew 3:6).

The gospel of salvation is all about receiving God's grace and mercy through being forgiven, but the Bible specifically says we have to confess our sins to receive His cleansing flow of mercy, *"If we confess our sins, [God] is faithful and just to forgive us our sins, and to cleanse us from all unrighteousness"* (1 John 1:9).

Unconfessed sin leaves a stain on one's conscience and provides an open door for Satan to work his ill-will in our lives. Proverb 5:22 says that we are bound and held with the cords of our iniquities. Confession cuts those cords, releasing us from Satan's bonds.

Quite naturally, the question arises, who should we confess to? Since all sin is an affront to God, we should first confess our sins directly to Him (see Psalm 51:34). Once we've obeyed the first step of the gospel and confessed to God, another important question arises, are there times when it is also necessary to confess to someone else, besides God? The answer to this question is a little more complex.

If, after we've confessed our trespasses to God our heart still isn't cleansed from guilt, then we must also confess to whoever we've trespassed against and ask for their forgiveness (see Matthew 5:23-24). Because of pride (and sometimes the fear of rejection), many people are reluctant to do this, and understandably so. It is much easier to humble ourselves to God than it is to someone we've wronged or offended. God already knows what we've done—we certainly aren't telling Him anything He doesn't already know!

Confessing to God is simply acknowledging the Holy Spirit's conviction and agreeing with Him that our selfish, sinful actions were wrong. Confessing to our neighbor and asking for his or her forgiveness is another matter altogether! It is truly humbling and carries the risk of rejection, which risk we have to accept as the inevitable consequence of our misdeeds.

Pride (and/or the fear of rejection) carries a stiff penalty. There are times when stubborn refusal to ask our neighbor's forgiveness will hinder our faith when we are faced with the need for healing. James said, *"Confess your trespasses to one another, and pray for one another, that you may be healed"* (James 5:16). It is difficult to believe God for healing when one has a guilty conscience!

Paul even said that unconfessed sin would follow one all the way to Christ's Judgment Seat and threaten one's eternal salvation: *"Some men's sins [have been repented of and properly confessed, so they] are clearly evident, preceding them to judgment, but those [unconfessed sins] of some men follow later [testifying against them on judgment day]. Likewise, the good works of some are clearly evident, and those that are otherwise cannot be hidden"* (1 Timothy 5:24-25). So, Paul states that both unconfessed sin and/or the lack of goods works (which manifest the validity of one's faith) will expose us to God's wrath on judgment day. Repentance and confession isn't a subject that should be taken lightly. Sin, especially unconfessed sin, is a very serious matter!

Today's church has failed to emphasize the need for sincere, heartfelt repentance. God wants us to be *baptized* into repentance, not just sprinkled. The very word translated baptize indicates immersion, not just getting a little wet by being sprinkled. In other words, God wants us to be completely immersed into repentance—and thereby throughly cleansed from the unrighteousness of sin—He doesn't want or accept insincere, half- hearted apologies.

# The Church Triumphant

Paul rebuked the Corinthian believers for not reproving the immorality that was going on in their midst but after they repented, he commended them with *"For godly sorrow produces repentance leading to salvation, not to be regretted; but the sorrow of the world produces death. For observe this very thing, that you sorrowed in a godly manner: What diligence it produced in you, what clearing of yourselves, what indignation, what fear, what vehement desire, what zeal, what vindication! In all things you proved yourselves to be clear in this matter"* (2 Corinthians 7:10-11).

God desires sincere, heartfelt repentance, and sometimes, when possible, He even requires us to make restitution for our trespasses before He will restore us to a state of blessedness. Instead of justifying ourselves, we should abhor ourselves and do everything we can to compensate others for the harm we've done to them (see Ezekiel 33:15-16; Job 42:5-6).

## The Baptism of Faith

Peter mentions the first two baptisms in his discussion of Noah's flood: *"There is also an antitype which now saves us— baptism (not the removal of the filth of the flesh, but the answer of a good conscience toward God), through the resurrection of Jesus Christ"* (1 Peter 3:21). When God warned Noah that He was going to destroy the world with a flood, Noah believed Him and built an ark, thereby saving his whole family. Peter observes that it wasn't the destruction of those who died that saved Noah, rather it was his faith. (Their death was symbolic of the baptism of repentance—God put away the filth of the flesh by drowning everyone except those who believed Noah's warning.) Noah's faith moved him to fear the coming judgment and his fear motivated him to obey (see Hebrews 11:7; James 2:22).

# The Church Triumphant

This *antitype* shows that although we must put away the filthiness of the flesh through repentance, repentance isn't what actually saves us—rather we are saved by *"the answer of a good conscience toward God, through the resurrection of Jesus Christ"*. God purifies our hearts by faith (see Acts 15:9; Hebrews 9:14). True, saving faith follows repentance.

This principle is seen in God's dealing with Abraham. *"Now the LORD had said to Abram: "Get out of your country, From your family And from your father's house, To a land that I will show you"* (Genesis 12:1). God said separate yourself from your country (cultural defilement), your family (any and all family ties that would prevent you from obeying God) and your father's house (all things, both tangible and intangible, that you may gain though your natural inheritance). Thus, one can see that true repentance involves far more than just turning away from sin. Everything in this world that would constitute dead works—even those things that are highly esteemed—must be laid aside to follow Christ (Philippians 3:7-8; Matthew 16:23).

Although the Bible says that Abraham *"believed in the LORD; and He counted it to him for righteousness"*, God's righteousness wasn't imputed unto him until after he had obeyed and left all to follow Him. Hebrews said, *"By faith Abraham, when he was called to go out into a place which he should after receive for an inheritance, obeyed; and he went out, not knowing whither he went"* (see Genesis 15:5-6; Hebrews 11:8). Just as it was in Noah's case, Abraham's faith was perfected by his obedience. One cannot be a true disciple of Christ and at the same time love and cling to the things of this world. Jesus said, *"So likewise, whoever of you does not forsake all that he has cannot be My disciple"* (Luke 14:33).

Our Heavenly Father is seeking a Bride for His Son that will separate herself from the world and love and follow Him with her whole heart. John cautioned, *"Do not love the world or the things in the world. If anyone loves the world, the love of the Father is not in him"* and Jesus explained why, *"For where your treasure is, there your heart will be also"* (see 1 John 2:15; Matthew 6:21).

## Water Baptism (The Baptism of Separation)

The third baptism, water baptism, is the one that most Christians are familiar with, although very few know why they are commanded to be baptized or what this baptism actually accomplishes. The most common reason given is that water baptism is *"an outward expression of an inward conversion"*. Although this answer may be true it isn't Biblical, nor does it explain why we should be baptized.

The simplest explanation of water baptism is this—sin is imputed by the law and water baptism separates our body from being under the law, thus "remitting" our sins. Paul said, *"For until the law [was given], sin was in the world: but sin is not imputed when there is no law"* (Romans 5:13; see also Colossians 2:11).

The most common objection to this is the belief that Gentiles aren't under the law. Although it is true that Gentiles are not under the letter of Moses' law, they *are* under the spirit of the law. Also, they are under God's eternal law that states *"Behold, all souls are Mine... The soul who sins shall die"* (Ezekiel 18:4). Also, Paul said, *"Now we know that whatever the law says, it says to those who are under the law, that every mouth may be stopped, and all the world [including Gentiles] may become guilty before God. Therefore by the deeds of the law no flesh will be justified in His sight, for by the law is the knowledge of sin"* (Romans 3:19-20). Thus we conclude that since we've all sinned—regardless of whether we are Jews under Moses' law or Gentiles under God's eternal law of sin and death—we are all under a death sentence. So, how do we escape? The answer is simple; instead of trying to escape we humbly agree with God that we are worthy of death and die with Christ! We repent!

When we believe the gospel and sincerely repent, we die to sin. Our death through repentance fulfills the righteous demands of the law, that the soul that sins must die. But, the law also requires the body of those who die by hanging on a tree to be buried. Thus when we die with Christ through repentance and are buried in water through water baptism, we fulfill and satisfy those two righteous demands of the law.

Observe Jesus' response to John when He came to be baptized. *"Then Jesus came... to John at the Jordan to be baptized by him. And John tried to prevent Him, saying, 'I need to be baptized by You, and are You coming to me?' But Jesus answered and said to him, 'Permit it to be so now, for thus it is fitting for us to fulfill all righteousness'."* (Matthew 3:13-16).

The law has dominion over our soul as long as we live and over our body until we are buried, but faith in Christ's death and resurrection imparts life to our spirit; dying in repentance delivers our soul from condemnation and water baptism sets our body free from the law. Once we are buried in water our body is free to be used of God because we are no longer under the law of sin and death but under the law of life in Christ Jesus (see Romans 6:13-14, 8:2).

Although water baptism is important, it isn't about eternal salvation as some teach, saying that if you aren't baptized in water correctly you are eternally doomed. Water baptism is about being physically, bodily, set free from the law so that Satan cannot use the curses found in the law against you while you living in this world. Satan uses the penalties imposed by Moses law to afflict mankind. Psalm 94:20 asks, *"Shall the throne of iniquity, which devises evil by law, have fellowship with You?"* Without the law, Satan is disarmed. Paul sums up this entire subject in his epistle to the Colossians:

> *In Him you were also circumcised with the circumcision made without hands, by putting off the body of the sins of the flesh, by the circumcision of Christ, buried with Him in [water] baptism, in which you also were raised with Him through faith in the working of God, who raised Him from the dead. And you, being dead in your trespasses and the uncircumcision of your flesh, He has made alive together with Him, having forgiven you all trespasses, having wiped out the handwriting of requirements that was against us, which was contrary to us. And He has taken it out of the way, having nailed it to the cross. Having disarmed principalities and powers, He made a public spectacle of them, triumphing over them in it* (Colossians 2:11-15).

Our spirit *is saved* by being born again through faith in the resurrection of Jesus Christ; our soul *is being saved* (sanctified) by faith and our body *will be saved* in the resurrection, but meanwhile, it is delivered from the demands and penalties of the law by water baptism. The thief on the Cross was saved without being water baptized. He repented and through *"the answer of a good conscience toward God"* received eternal life (see Luke 23:39-43).

So, should we be baptized? Yes, as Peter said, *"Then Peter said to them, "Repent, and let every one of you be baptized in the name of Jesus Christ for the remission of sins; and you shall receive the [next baptism, which is the] gift of the Holy Spirit'."* (Acts 2:38). And how should one be baptized? As Peter said in the verse above, by immersion in the Name of Jesus Christ (see Colossians 3:17; Acts 8:6, 10:48, 19:5; Romans 6:3).

## Holy Spirit Baptism

The forth baptism—the baptism of the Holy Spirit—has been, and still is, the most controversial of them all. Satan hates this baptism because it is his nemesis. I'm sure that his initial response to the outpouring of the Holy Spirit upon the early church was, *"Oh No! Here comes the Judge!"* Why? Because Jesus promised that when the Holy Spirit came He would reprove the world of sin, righteousness and judgment... *because the prince of this world is judged* (see John 16:8-11). Satan is judged and his deceptions are exposed!

Satan hid in the shadows until God's light revealed his evil presence. *"God is light and in Him is no darkness at all"* (1 John 1:5). God is a Spirit and His Spirit is light! Satan is darkness and light always dispels darkness. This is one rule that has no exceptions.

Without the baptism of the Holy Spirit the church is in darkness and is unable to judge properly. Notice the confusion and ill-advised actions taken by some of the mainline denominations concerning ordaining homosexual priests and performing gay marriages. They are blind and cannot see the simple truth as it is revealed in Scripture because they have rejected the Light. Instead of reproving homosexuality, as Paul commanded us to do in Ephesians 5:3,11, they openly condone it and in many ways, actually cause it! Homosexuality is caused by rejecting the experiential knowledge of God, which they have done by rejecting the baptism of the Holy Spirit.

The Holy Spirit's attributes and work can be seen by examining some of the many names by which He is called. Jesus called Him, *the Spirit of Truth* and *the Comforter* (see John 15:26).

# The Church Triumphant

Paul called Him, *the Spirit of Holiness* and *the Spirit of Adoption*, also, *the Spirit of Promise* and *the Spirit of God* (see Romans 1:4, 8:15; Ephesians 1:13, 4:30). The writer of Hebrews called Him, *the Spirit of Grace* and Zechariah added, *the Spirit of Supplications* (see Hebrews 10:29; Zechariah 12:10). And one might say Peter summed it all up by calling Him, *the Spirit of Glory* (see 1 Peter 4:14). That is a pretty impressive array of attributes and that is only a partial list!

The Holy Spirit baptism is available to anyone who sincerely asks, but you do have to ask! Jesus said, *"If ye then, being evil, know how to give good gifts unto your children: how much more shall your heavenly Father give the Holy Spirit to them that ask him?"* (Luke 11:13). We receive not because we ask not. The Holy Spirit is too valuable and wonderful a gift to go thorough life without simply because we neglected to ask God for it!

Paul said that we are (or should be) *"sealed with the Holy Spirit of Promise, who is the guarantee of our inheritance"* (see Ephesians 1:13-14). This baptism and its nine manifestations are both a witness to us and to the world that we truly are covenant children of God! (see Hebrews 2:4, 10:15-17; 1 Corinthians 12:4-11). Without the Holy Spirit baptism and numerous manifestations we are powerless to give the world any real, concrete evidence of God's presence.

Jesus said the Holy Spirit teaches us all things, shows us things to come and reveals the heavenly things of both the Father and the Son to us. Also, that He would bring to our remembrance whatever Christ told us. The Holy Spirit opens both God's Word to our hearts and our hearts to His word! (see John 14:26, 16:13-15; Acts 16:14). Is it any wonder that Satan hates this baptism?

# The Church Triumphant

## The Baptism of Fire (Part I)

The fifth and sixth baptisms, the two baptisms of fire, have long been awaited by the church, although very few know what they are actually waiting for—and even fewer know what to expect once this baptism arrives! This is a two-in-one baptism—actually, two baptisms with one name—as seen in the *"divided tongues, as of fire"* of Acts 2:3. This baptism releases tremendous power, but as John clearly stated in Luke 3:16-17, it also purifies everyone it falls upon: (*"He will baptize you with the Holy Spirit and fire. His winnowing fan is in His hand, and He will thoroughly clean out His threshing floor, and gather the wheat into His barn; but the chaff He will burn with unquenchable fire"*). These two, power and purification, are inseparable. God's powerful, consuming fire burns away every impurity that doesn't conform to the image of Christ.

Once we have fully obeyed the gospel of salvation—that is, we have died to this world through repentance, been separated from the law through water baptism and arose from the dead through faith in Christ's resurrection—our Covenant with God is ratified and sealed by the Holy Spirit baptism, transforming us into living witnesses of Jesus' resurrection. As a result our limited fruitfulness through the Holy Spirit baptism—in His discourse on the Vine and the branches—Jesus promised, *"Every branch in me that bears not fruit he takes away: and every branch that bears fruit, he purges it, that it may bring forth more fruit"* (see John 15:1-2). *Purges* in this verse is translated from the Greek word *kathairo* and is derived from *katharos*, which means to *cleanse*.

God's chosen instrument for scrubbing His clay vessels is *fire*, as in Isaiah 4:4: *"the Lord has washed away the filth of the daughters of Zion... by the spirit of judgment and by the spirit of burning"*. Likewise, Jesus assured us that every disciple of His would be *"salted with fire"* (see Mark 9:49). The evidence of this fire is all around us. It is everywhere you look. Almost everyone in ministry is presently undergoing tremendous pressure as they walk in Jesus' footsteps in preparation for the glorious times we are entering into.

At one point Jesus remarked, *"I have a baptism to be baptized with, and how distressed I am till it is accomplished!"* (Luke 12:50). *Distressed* is from the Greek word *synecho* and means to be *"perplexed from being placed under extreme agony and mental duress"*.

Many Christians are perplexed as they ponder the fiery trial they are enduring at this time. As John said in Luke 3:17, God's fire is unquenchable. We cannot extinguish it by praying for relief. It burns until it accomplishes its purpose, which is nothing less than willing obedience. The Bible says that although Jesus was God's Son, *"yet He learned obedience by the things which He suffered"* (Hebrews 5:8). We, too, are destined to suffer the same fate—God doesn't play favorites. But don't despair, God has a purpose in all that we are being put through. We have the promise of better days ahead. Peter promised, *"Beloved, do not think it strange concerning the fiery trial which is to try you, as though some strange thing happened to you [for] after you have suffered a while [God will], perfect, establish, strengthen, and settle you"* (see 1 Peter 4:12, 5:10).

The first half of this twofold baptism is thrilling, resurrection power! Earth shaking, devil stomping, sin destroying, life changing, soul saving, body healing, miracle working, attention demanding, supernatural power. Notice that John prophesied that along with the fire Christ would *"gather the wheat into His barn"*. Besides instant, visible miracles of healing, there is also an unprecedented harvest of souls predestined to be saved, especially among the young. But the second half of the baptism of fire is not so thrilling—it is purification. It is to make us worthy to *"Give unto the LORD the glory due to His name [and to] Worship the LORD in the beauty of holiness"* (Psalm 29:2).

## The Baptism of Fire (Part II)

As we've discussed, the fifth and sixth baptism consists of two inseparable baptisms with only one name—the baptism of fire. They are administered simultaneously because both release supernatural, resurrection power. Since the same power that raises the dead will also kill the living, this twofold baptism administers both life and death, whichever is needed to accomplish God's purposes at any given time. Its purpose is to first sever our attachment to the world, then give us power over the prince of this world—as Paul said in Galatians— *"God forbid that I should boast except in the cross of our Lord Jesus Christ, by whom the world has been crucified to me, and I to the world."* and in Romans, *"And the God of peace will crush Satan under your feet shortly"* (Galatians 6:14; Romans 16:20).

The first four baptisms crucify the *world* to us and separates us from the world, *but the baptism of fire crucifies us to the world and separates the world from us!* It first crucifies our inordinate affection for the things of this world and then empowers us to rule over the *"prince of the power of the air, the spirit who now works in the sons of disobedience"* (Ephesians 2:2). This baptism was never designed to make us popular with those who love the world!

Besides being cast into God's purifying fire, how does one know that he or she has received the baptism of fire? The answer is quite simple. Our spiritual, three day journey of faith consists of three individual stages, in which we walk with our words. In every case public *speech* is the initial manifestation, or evidence, that we have begun the next phase of our journey, as Paul said: *"we have the same spirit of faith, according to what is written, 'I believed and therefore I spoke,' we also believe and therefore speak"* (see 2 Corinthians 4:13; Exodus 3:18).

Initially, we start our journey by publicly confessing and acknowledging Jesus as our Lord and Savior. Then, somewhere along the way we experience the baptism of the Holy Spirit with the initial evidence of speaking in other tongues. Then we enter the third and last stage, which is undoubtedly the hardest and most challenging of all. This stage is where many fall away and turn back to the world, as Paul's fellow laborer Demas did when he forsook Paul and left him when he was in prison. Paul advised Timothy that *"Demas has forsaken me, having loved this present world"* (see Philemon 1:24; 2 Timothy 4:10).

But those who endure and *"follow on to know the Lord"*, as Hosea 6:2-3 says, know they've experienced the baptism of fire by the bold, uncompromising testimony and speech that freely and often spontaneously flows from their mouths—even when threatened with persecution. In the same way that the baptism of the Holy Spirit is the fulfillment of the Feast of Pentecost, the baptism of fire corresponds to the next feast, the Feast of Trumpets. In Scripture, bold speech is compared to a trumpet's blast, as when Isaiah commanded Israel to *"Cry aloud, spare not; Lift up your voice like a trumpet; Tell My people their transgression, And the house of Jacob their sins"* (Isaiah 58:1).

When the early church was threatened with persecution they prayed in unison and experienced a divine outpouring of supernatural power. The following passage of Scripture describes the second release of the baptism of fire and illustrates three of its primary attributes: *"And when they had prayed, the place where they were assembled together was shaken; and they were all filled with the Holy Spirit, and they spoke the word of God with boldness. And the multitude of them that believed were of one heart and of one soul: neither said any of them that ought of the things which he possessed was his own; but they had all things common. And with great power gave the apostles witness of the resurrection of the Lord Jesus: and great grace was upon them all"* (Acts 4:31-33).

God graciously empowered them to boldly witness in open defiance of the civil authorities' demands. He also broke any affection for the things of this world and granted many powerful, miraculous signs and wonders to be done by the apostles' hands.

As I mentioned in the Baptism of Fire, Part I, the first outpouring of this baptism occurred on the day of Pentecost, illustrated by the *"divided tongues, as of fire"*, that *"sat on each of them"*. The fact that all of them received it shows that this baptism is for everyone, not just for a select few. Jesus confirmed this when He stated *"**everyone** will be salted with fire"* (see Acts 2:3; Mark 9:49).

This two part baptism is now on God's agenda for the church. As with every new move of God, this one won't be heartily welcomed by lukewarm Christians who are comfortable in their ways or desire to hold on to their age-old religious traditions. Although many will gladly embrace the powerful healing miracles that accompany it, when it comes to sacrificing the refinements of this world that they've grown so accustomed to enjoying, such as sterling reputations and abundant material possessions, it will be met with much trepidation and resistance. It will be far too upsetting, especially in America's materialistic, idolatrous society.

Idolatrous people are spiritual but not godly, religious but not holy. There are many who profess Jesus as savior that are actually enemies of the Cross of Christ (see Philippians 3:18-19). This powerful baptism will draw a line of demarcation before them and force them to make a decision to either surrender all for Christ or turn back to Egypt, from whence they came.

## The Baptism of Suffering and (Willing) Sacrifice

Paul said we are predestined to be conformed to the image of Christ (see Romans 8:29). Jesus led the way and set the example. Hebrews says, *"though He was a Son, yet He learned obedience by the things which He suffered. **And having been perfected**, He became the author of eternal salvation to all who obey Him"* (Hebrews 5:8-9). Maturity (perfection) is an attribute of character. Like tempered steel, godly character is forged in the furnace of affliction.

Suffering severs our affections for the things of this world, and this is one of the primary purposes of the baptism of suffering. John said, *"Love not the world, neither the things that are in the world. If any man loves the world, the love of the Father is not in him"* (1 John 2:15).

Jesus said that even loving one's own family members more than Him disqualifies us from partaking of His eternal kingdom: *"He who loves father or mother more than Me is not worthy of Me. And he who loves son or daughter more than Me is not worthy of Me. And he who does not take his cross and follow after Me is not worthy of Me"* (Matthew 10:37-38).

This is seen in God's dealings with Abraham when He told him to leave his father's house and sojourn with Him in a strange land, which He promised to give to his descendants. Also, here we see an inherent principal imbedded in the gospel covenant. God always promises us an eternal (not temporary) reward for our obedience. The eternal versus temporary aspect of this reward is seen in the fact that Abraham only sojourned in the land; he never personally owned it:

Stephen makes this point in his final address to his persecutors right before they stoned him: *"And God gave [Abraham] no inheritance in it, not even enough to set his foot on... [yet] He promised to give it to him for a possession, and to his descendants after him"* (Acts 7:4-5). Thus it is clear that the promise of inheritance was a future, eternal promise, not one that was immediate and temporary.

Why is it of vital importance that we understand this principal of eternal reward? Because obedience to the gospel of the kingdom requires us to leave this world and its goods to those who are "of this world" and take up our cross of self-denial and follow Christ. Our strength to endure the pain of persecution and the high cost of sacrifice and service comes only by looking beyond the cross to the promised crown of glory (see 1 Peter 5:4; Hebrews 12:2).

Even Moses was motivated by the reward that he saw through the eyes of faith: *"By faith Moses... refused to be called the son of Pharaoh's daughter, choosing rather to suffer affliction with the people of God than to enjoy the passing pleasures of sin, esteeming the reproach of Christ greater riches than the treasures in Egypt; for he looked to the reward"* (Hebrews 11:24-26). And when Paul spoke of the promised resurrection with its accompanying rewards, he said, *"If in this life only we have hope in Christ, we are of all men the most pitiable"* (1 Corinthians 15:19). Faith in God's faithfulness is the one thing that enables us to endure the suffering of this last and final baptism, the baptism of willing suffering and sacrifice.

This is God's ultimate purpose in all His dealings with us as He, through fiery trials, conforms us into the image of His Son—so that we, without complaint—willingly serve, cheerfully give and patiently endure the fellowship of His sufferings. As Israel was called out of Egypt to follow Moses on a three day journey into the wilderness and sacrifice, we, too, are called to go out of this world on a three day journey to offer a sacrifice to God (see Exodus 3:18). It's been a long, arduous journey. As we approach the evening of the third and last day, it's time to offer the evening sacrifice. That sacrifice is our life,

> *I beseech you therefore, brethren, by the mercies of God, that you present your bodies a living sacrifice, holy, acceptable to God, which is your reasonable service. And do not be conformed to this world, but be transformed by the renewing of your mind, that you may prove what is that good and acceptable and perfect will of God* (Romans 12:1-2)

# Bibliography

THE GOSPEL OF THE KINGDOM, *George Eldon Ladd, William B. Eerdmans Publishing Company, 1959*

THE FOUR WINDS, *Ira L. Milligan, Servant Ministries, Inc., 2013*

THE SEVEN MOUNTAIN MANTLE, Johnny Enlow, Creation House, 2009

THE HOUSE CHURCH BOOK, Wolfgang Simson, Tyndale House Publishers, 2009

## The Ultimate Guide to Understanding the Dreams You Dream

*Biblical Keys for Hearing God's Voice in the Night*

*The Ultimate Guide to Understanding the Dreams You Dream* provides insight into your nighttime experiences—and your life! Also included is a comprehensive dictionary of dream symbols to guide you through the complex world of dreams.

Best-selling author and minister Ira Milligan has decades of personal experience receiving, understanding and interpreting dreams of his own and those of others. He uses biblical examples to illustrate the way God uses dreams to communicate to His people. This book gives you *Biblical Keys for Hearing God's Voice in the Night* through:

- Specific, detailed directions about meditation and hearing God's voice.
- A comprehensive A-Z dictionary of symbol definitions.
- Discerning the difference between God-given dreams and those received from other sources. Both normal and not-so-normal dream situations are presented, giving you the basis for interpreting your own dreams.

# *Servant Ministries Inc.*

To order directly from the internet, go to:
www.servant-ministries.org

---

To obtain a complete price list of books available from
*Servant Ministries, Inc.*, copy, complete and mail the
information in the form below. (Please print)

Name: _____

Address: _____

City: _____

State: _____ Zip: _____

Ph. No. ( _____ ) _____

Mail this form to:
**Servant Ministries, Inc.**
PO Box 1120 − Tioga, LA 71477